Blessing
the Animals

Another SkyLight Paths book
edited by Lynn L. Caruso

Honoring Motherhood:
Prayers, Ceremonies and Blessings

Blessing
the Animals

Prayers and Ceremonies
to Celebrate
God's Creatures, Wild and Tame

Edited and with Introductions by
Lynn L. Caruso

Walking Together, Finding the Way®
SKYLIGHT PATHS®
PUBLISHING
Nashville, Tennessee

Blessing the Animals:
Prayers and Ceremonies to Celebrate God's Creatures, Wild and Tame

Library of Congress Cataloging-in-Publication Data
Blessing the animals : prayers and ceremonies to celebrate God's creatures, wild and tame / edited and with introductions by Lynn L. Caruso.
p. cm.
ISBN-13: 978-1-59473-145-7 (hardcover)
ISBN-10: 1-59473-145-4 (hardcover)
1. Animals—Religious aspects—Meditations. 2. Prayers for animals.
3. Benediction. I. Caruso, Lynn L., 1968–
BL439.B54 2006
203'.8—dc22

2005030417

ISBN-13: 978-1-59473-253-9 (quality pbk.)
ISBN-10: 1-59473-253-1 (quality pbk.)

Manufactured in the United States of America
Cover Design: Sara Dismukes
Illustrations: Sara Dismukes
SkyLight Paths, "Walking Together, Finding the Way," and colophon are trademarks of LongHill Partners, Inc., registered in the U.S. Patent and Trademark Office.

SkyLight Paths Publishing is creating a place where people of different spiritual traditions come together for challenge and inspiration, a place where we can help each other understand the mystery that lies at the heart of our existence.

SkyLight Paths sees both believers and seekers as a community that increasingly transcends traditional boundaries of religion and denomination—people wanting to learn from each other, walking together, finding the way.

Walking Together, Finding the Way®
Published by SkyLight Paths Publishing
An imprint of Turner Publishing Company
4507 Charlotte Avenue, Suite 100
Nashville, TN 37209
Tel: (655) 255-2665
www.skylightpaths.com

To my sons
Isaac, Samuel, and little Eli—
whose journey is just beginning.
And to Patrick, for your enduring love.

Contents

Part 4

Rituals and Ceremonies

Introduction

Years ago, two friends and I spent several days backpacking in the Olympic National Rainforest in Washington State. We chose the twenty-mile loop trail through the lush Hoh River Valley to Bogachiel Peak because of the amazing panoramic views we were promised by others who had made the trip. But nearing the summit, our enthusiasm paled with the realization that this lofty peak, large enough for our small tent and little else, was surrounded, like an island, by thick clouds. Everything—the other mountains in the Olympic Range, the alpine lake below, even the trail we had just climbed—everything was hidden.

Just moments after my friends disappeared in search of water, an enormous black-tailed buck stepped up through the fog and stood beside my tent. Staring out over the clouds and the setting sun, he was aware that I was there, but hardly acknowledged my presence. It was, after all, his mountain, and it would remain his long after I stuffed my tent back into its nylon sack and wound my way to the valley floor below.

Then suddenly the clouds shifted and began to drop, almost as if the sun were melting them and dragging them along in her wake as she slid toward the horizon. One by one the peaks appeared, and then the Seven Lakes Basin and the Pacific Ocean — a stroke of blue at the edge of the world. To this day I can't believe there wasn't music — loud angelic choirs, a timpani, a brass horn — something. And all the while the buck just stood beside my tent, watching in silence. *Is this what it's like every night on your mountain?* I wanted to ask. *Is the world created again and again at the close of every day?* But I couldn't speak. At that moment, the buck disappeared over the cliff's edge and down to the glacier field below.

Even now, my attempts to describe this experience fall short. There were colors that have never been named, and a light I've seen only at my son's birth. It is this experience that lies at the heart of this book. A sacred moment of connection between human and animal. A moment when we fully meet another member of creation. The Jewish philosopher Martin Buber described such experiences as moments of true meeting — where we approach another not as subject and object, as I-It, but as mutual subjects, I-Thou. Buber wrote that when we open ourselves up to such experiences, we gain a "glimpse through to the Eternal Thou." Such moments of encounter are experienced again and again throughout the pages of this book, captured in the bark of Feng Chih's puppy or the soul's weight of Alicia Hokanson's cat.

This book is a collection of poems, prayers, and blessings from many faiths. Within these pages are blessings for animals, both companion and wild, as well as writings that explore the blessings we receive from animals. The book concludes with several original multifaith ceremonies to be conducted with animals throughout life's passages.

Humankind is only one of a multitude of species that inhabit this wild planet. Yet we often consider the world and all its inhabitants to have been created expressly for us. The writings in this collection portray an image of a Creator who cares compassionately for all members of creation. The fifteenth-century Indian mystic Kabir writes that the Lord can hear even the "subtle anklets that ring on the feet of an insect when it moves." And in Genesis, we read that God created animals with the same breath as humans, blessed them, and declared them good. Their blessing was not conditional upon any relation to us. Animals possess their own intrinsic worth and goodness, their own unique map of experiences. Twentieth-century Roman Catholic theologian Hans Urs von Balthasar wrote, "The whole point of creation, is for us to know that we are not Creator."

We are not Creator, yet we are undeniably connected to all of creation. There is a two-word Lakota Sioux prayer, "Mitakuye Oyasin," which translates as "All My

Relations." This prayer of oneness emphasizes our kinship with all forms of creation in the sacred hoop of life. This echoing chord of interconnectedness runs throughout the score of this book, and with recognition of kinship comes responsibility. If we open ourselves up, as the writers in this book have done, to the possibility of reciprocal blessings between humans and animals, then we must be ever mindful that any endangered or extinct animal, any destruction to our fragile environment, disturbs the harmony of the whole.

Included in these pages are voices that represent a wide range of faith traditions, yet there is a surprising convergence as all join together in honoring animals. My experience on Bogachiel Peak remains one of the most spiritual encounters of my life. Standing beside that buck as the clouds fell and the world appeared below us—experiencing it all together—was one of my life's sacred I-Thou connections.

The writers in *Blessing the Animals* have eloquently given voice to their own sacred connections with animals, recapturing for us a language that much of creation seems never to have forgotten. I invite you to explore the writings in this collection in search of your own spiritual encounters with all God's creatures—expecting the blessings to resonate beyond the final benediction.

Part 1

Blessings for Companion Animals

Some of my earliest and most vivid memories of childhood involve a companion that spoke most profoundly with tail and tongue. From Reed's first days as a puppy being paraded around in an antique baby carriage, through years as my faithful running partner, until that final moment when I had to make the painful decision to end his suffering, we shared a relationship that could only be described as friendship—raw, unselfish, undeniable friendship. The pieces included in this section capture the intimacy of our relationships with dogs, cats, and other companion and domestic animals. They explore the blessings and mystery inherent in these relationships and recognize the possibility for true friendship.

Throughout history, and across all faith traditions, there are accounts of spiritual connections with companion animals. One of the earliest forms of religious worship was that of animal worship in ancient Egypt. Egyptians viewed dogs and cats as sacred, erecting a temple to their cat deity, the goddess Bast, and upholding the relationship between dogs and humans as an ideal representation of the relationship between an individual and his or her God. These early civilizations believed there was something mysterious, holy, and certainly worth blessing in these companions.

Both the Hindu teachings of Sri Ramakrishna and those of Jesus in the Christian Bible provide similar metaphors for the relationship an individual should seek with the Creator. Hindu followers are called to love God with the same devotion that a mother cat has for her kittens, while the compassion of shepherds for their sheep is presented as an example of the relationship Jesus had with his followers. There is an inherent reverence and respect bestowed upon an animal when it is held up in such holy light.

Jewish philosopher Martin Buber recommended that we should approach the world around us — whether people, animals, plants, or even a mountain of stones — in a relationship of I-Thou. It is doubtful that our relationships with the animal world would have developed beyond that of human and wild, subject and object, if we had failed to approach all of creation with this reverential attitude — if instead we chose to treat all animals as mere objects of our dominion. Buber asserted that, ultimately, all real life happens in relationship, when we mutually connect with another.

The writers in this section have given words to such moments of encounter, but I'm certain many of them would maintain that what matters most is not the perfect metaphor or eloquent description, but the relationship itself. Robert Bly wrote that "every poet should take care of animals as part of her or his preparation." And the writings on these pages are certainly imbued with more compassion, more wonder and beauty, because of such relationships.

I once received a phone call in the middle of the night from a friend who was in her final days of a devastating battle with breast cancer. She was worried about what would happen to her beloved dog when she was no longer able to care for him, and her worry was keeping her up at night. This friend was one of the most spiritual people I have ever known, and it was no surprise that at the end of her life she was concerned with the care of her companion. There was nothing sentimental about this relationship but rather something real, reciprocal, and spiritual. It was a relationship that clearly brought blessings of unconditional love and devotion to both.

Whether through a mutual glance or a bark that fills our darkest days with light, anyone who has experienced a companion relationship with an animal knows the possibility for rich blessings. It is my hope that the writings in this chapter serve as a reciprocal blessing—addressing each animal as "Thou" and providing a glimpse through to the Eternal Thou as we travel on this spiritual migration together, companions in the wildness of creation.

1 *Blessings for Dogs*

SONNET TWENTY-THREE
[ON A PUPPY]

Rain has fallen continuously for half a month;
Since you were born
You've only known the dismal, the gloomy.
One day, rain clouds suddenly disperse

and sunlight beams over the wall.
I see your mother then,
Lifting you in her jaws to the sunrays

Letting you feel the light and warmth for the first
  time.
And at sunset, she brings you
in again. You haven't

a memory, but the experience
will manifest itself, when some day you'll
bark and bring forth light in the dark of night.

Feng Chih, translated by Dominic Cheung

GOLDEN RETRIEVALS

Fetch? Balls and sticks capture my attention
seconds at a time. Catch? I don't think so.
Bunny, tumbling leaf, a squirrel who's—oh
joy—actually scared. Sniff the wind, then

I'm off again: muck, pond, ditch, residue
of any thrillingly dead thing. And you?
Either you're sunk in the past, half our walk,
thinking of what you never can bring back,

or else you're off in some fog concerning
—tomorrow, is that what you call it? My work:
to unsnare time's warp (and woof!), retrieving,
my haze-headed friend, you. This shining bark,

a Zen master's bronzy gong, calls you here,
entirely, now: bow-wow, bow-wow, bow-wow.

Mark Doty

REFLECTION ON THE WRITINGS OF ZEN MASTER CHAO-CHOU TS'UNG-SHEN

All sentient beings do in fact have Buddha-nature, dogs included, but ... they need to wake up to the fact if it is to do them any good. The "road that leads to Ch'ang-an" may run in front of every house, but unless one actually travels it, the sights and smells of the capital can only be imagined.

T. Griffith Foulk

God, bless the animals, and especially the dog. Dogs are willing, even anxious, to love us. Help us to be willing and anxious also, God, to love them and to love one another. Dogs illustrate for us how to be loyal, faithful, playful, creative, intelligent, tenacious, steadfast, and most of all forgiving. Dogs, if we let them be, are among your most patient and gentle teachers. God, thank You for dogs—for the gifts they bring, the lessons they teach, the joy of life they exhibit. Bless the dogs of our planet, God—everywhere. Amen.

Rev. Lauren McLaughlin

The Prophet said, "A man felt very thirsty while he was on the way, there he came across a well. He went down the well, quenched his thirst and came out. Meanwhile he saw a dog panting and licking mud because of excessive thirst. He said to himself, 'This dog is suffering from thirst as I did.' So, he went down the well again and filled his shoe with water and watered it. Allah thanked him for that deed and forgave him. The people said, 'O Allah's Apostle! Is there a reward for us in serving the animals?' He replied: 'Yes, there is a reward for serving any animate [living being].'"

Bukhari Hadith 3:646

PRAISE

I heard the dogs before
I opened the door late, after work —
first Maude who was dancing
in praise of my arrival for all she knew
it was: presence without end,
the end of waiting, the end
of boredom —
        and then Li Po,
who, in the middle of his life,
learning to make his feelings known
as one who has carried breath
and heart close to the earth seven
times seven years, in praise
of silence and loneliness, climbed
howling, howling from his bed.

Laurie Lamon

With my hand upon his head,
Is my benediction said, therefore, and forever.
Blessings on thee, dog of mine,
Pretty collars make thee fine,
Sugared milk make fat thee!
Pleasures wag on in thy tail —
Hands of gentle motion fail
Nevermore, to pat thee!

Yet be blessed to the height
Of all good and all delight
Pervious to thy nature.
Only *loved* beyond that line,
With a love that answer thine,
Loving fellow-creature!

Elizabeth Barrett Browning, from
"To Flush, My Dog"

THE DOG'S JOB

Who assigned you this task, Mr. Big Boy,
Shaky Legs, Bony Old Fur Bag,
to bark me from bed with your booming voice
at 3 a.m. in the middle of winter?

You're off down the hall with your shuffling gait,
trailing tufts of white hair that float up like
    milkweed.
I stumble after, yawning, cursing,
eyes out of focus, a catch in my knee —
I'm not such a puppy myself now, you know.

Grumbling slave to your impatient bladder,
I clutch at my robe against what is coming
and roll aside the patio door.
Together we lurch out over the sill,
smack into the cold
and the crystalline dark and
oh my god
the stars.

Rivage

Dog, n. A kind of additional or subsidiary Deity designed to catch the overflow and surplus of the world's worship.

Ambrose Bierce

∼

The dog was created especially for children. He is the god of frolic.

Henry Ward Beecher

∼

I have sometimes thought of the final cause of dogs having such short lives and I am quite satisfied it is in compassion to the human race; for if we suffer so much in losing a dog after an acquaintance of ten or twelve years, what would it be if they were to live double that time?

Sir Walter Scott

LOST ALLELUIA: SOME FRAGMENTS FROM PSALM 23 FOUND

In tribute to my pet, Alleluia

On a chandelier-clear plateau,
   in Mountains called Rocky.
   a summer camp swayed like a pendulum
   full of time and children
   where I was counselor
Before my own children were born,
Nine thousand feet high into the giant blank sky.
     And
My young yapping collie pup, born and bred in
     the city,
By herding
Played
With them.

Then just before dinner, word, simmering, came
That Ollie was not coming, was missing from
     dinner, and
From everything.

Without notice or trace, my collie had strayed
   into red arroyos of quietness,
   into canyons that cannot echo,
   into silence that devours.

Hear only the long-spurred cerulean flower's
　　stem aching as it arcs.
Hear only the blade of grass
　　sharpening.
Hear only the groan of earth
　　bearing up
　　under the biting needles of the sucking sap-
　　　　filled pine tree.

The silence under the cool metallic sun
　　on the green alpine meadows called Black Mesa
　　is quite palpable in Colorado.
The silence keeps its secrets hidden
　　in the hardiness of the forest during the day, and
　　in the illusoriness of the craggy woods at night.

The silence is instead of air.

I imagine my dog dead in a cave during the
　　　　crystal day,
　　and during the onyx night
　　freezing, bleeding, under bushes frightened
　　　　by predators
　　and their desultory noises.
I cry her name, "Alleluia," "Ali,"
　　again and again and again.
The thin wind swallows my voice;
The thin wind makes ghosts of everything,
　　even of the child-like aspen.

One more time I cry Alleluia
   before it makes a ghost of me.

At the end of the third day, I abandon the search.

A fortnight later, a fisherman phones
   responding to my newspaper notice;
   and he tells me he noticed
   a thin dog
   with a thorn in her paw,
   drinking water near his fishing rod spot,
   fitting my description;
   and he has carried her by car to his garage.
I, beyond belief, silence broken, tell him
   "I will come right away."

Two hundred miles each way I drive
   to retrieve my mange-coated, ribs-showing,
      barely breathing
   collie plucked wheezing from
   the shadowy vales of silence.

I rejoice to provide a bounty of two hundred
      dollars for the reading angler in
      Montrose, and
   a bounty of cups and weeping for my puppy,
   anointing her head with oil, raising alleluias.

                                   John C. Chendo

I am quite sure he thinks that I am God—
Since He is God on whom each one depends
For life, and all things that His bounty sends—
My dear old dog, most constant of all friends;
Not quick to mind, but quicker far than I
To Him whom God I know and own: his eye
Deep brown and liquid, watches for my nod;
…
He looks love at me, deep as words e'er spake;
And from me never crumb or sup will take
But he wags thanks with his most vocal tail;
And when some crashing noise wakes all his fear
He is content and quiet if I'm near,
Secure that my protection will prevail;
So, faithful, mindful, thankful, trustful, he
Tells me what I unto my God should be.

Bishop George Washington Doane

O, heavenly Father, protect and bless all things
    that have breath;
guard them from all evil,
and let them sleep in peace.

Albert Schweitzer

Recollect that the Almighty, who gave the dog
to be companion of our pleasures and toils,
hath invested him with a nature noble and
incapable of deceit.

Sir Walter Scott, from The Talisman

2 Blessings for Cats

Oh wisdom
in your fur coat
and whiskers.
What don't you know?
Sometimes I believe
I have seen my soul searched
in your eyes,
how much time passes
between us without word?
How much do you know
that I've just begun
to understand?

Spirit of grace and humor
on all fours.

Pam Reinke

Sri Ramakrishna prefaces this passage by saying, "Love God even as the mother loves her child."

It is necessary to pray to Him with a longing heart. The kitten knows only how to call its mother, crying, "Mew, mew!" It remains satisfied wherever its mother puts it. And the mother cat puts the kitten sometimes in the kitchen, sometimes on the floor, and sometimes on the bed. When it suffers it cries only, "Mew, mew!" That's all it knows. But as soon as the mother hears this cry, wherever she may be, she comes to the kitten.

Sri Ramakrishna

AN OLD RUSSIAN PRAYER

Hear our prayer, Lord, for all animals,
May they be well-fed and well-trained and
    happy;
Protect them from hunger and fear and suffering;
And, we pray, protect specially, dear Lord,
The little cat who is the companion of our home,
Keep her safe as she goes abroad,
And bring her back to comfort us.

Author unknown

One day Muhammad was reading from the holy Qur'an to a group of followers when his beloved cat, Muezza, fell asleep on the sleeve of his robe. When the time came for the Prophet to leave, he took a knife and cut the sleeve from his robe, destroying his fine robe yet leaving the sleeping cat undisturbed.

Retelling of Islamic folk story

The love we give to a pet, and receive from a pet, can draw us more deeply into the larger circle of life, into the wonder of our common relationship to our Creator.

Kevin E. Mackin, OFM

~

And in looking through God's great stone books made up of records reaching back millions and millions of years, it is a great comfort to learn that vast multitudes of creatures, great and small and infinite in number, lived and had a good time in God's love before man was created.

John Muir, from "Cats and Dogs"

ESSAY ON COMPASSION

After Stephen Dunn's "From Underneath"

The cat wound tight against my foot idles himself
    to sleep
I tell myself he loves me past food and shelter
past my fingers' rough massage

I think I know this to be true but say *I tell myself*
to show how carefully I assume nothing
to prove I am no sentimental fool

When I cut my hand this same cat lapped
the blood that pooled like cooling grease
but when I cried for what I thought was loss

of what again I'd thought was love
he touched my cheek with one dry paw
stared into my eyes until I looked away

The newspaper says a giant sea turtle
carried a shipwrecked woman most of two days
before delivering her up to a fishing boat

How to explain the turtle's choice
that it rose beneath the woman twice
before she let herself ride that cold back

that in two days the turtle did not once dive
How would a biologist dismiss this as
some odd coincidence of instincts

the woman saved without the turtle caring
I say and mostly do not trust that the turtle
saved her life because it wanted to

I say too with all the certainty of one
who never made or saved a life
this must have been compassion

that well fed in calm salt water one turtle
had no stronger thirst that day than to try on
a cast off human goodness to see if it would float

When this deaf and aged slack ribbed cat
gets up to walk his bones across the room
stops and seems to slowly reconsider

then limps back to where he'd started
I think it better for us all that I assume
that when he seems to think he thinks

that when he seems to love he loves
that the turtle knew exactly what it did
and what would happen if it didn't

Richard Lehnert

God, bless the animals, especially the cat. We love our domestic cats, God, and admire them for their independence and their innate self-respect. We are fascinated by their infinite curiosity and natural unpredictability. Wild cats awaken in us a sense of magic and mystery. They have such an amazing ability to be at home in the dark. Grant us, God, some of those character traits that we so admire in Your cats. Remind us that You created us also to be free and independent creatures, and that it would serve us well to be more willing to express our own natural curiosity. Lead us to the best methods of protecting our earth to make it safe and comfortable for Your wild cats, God, and strengthen in us our resolve to nurture and protect Your domestic cats from disease and overpopulation. Thank You, God, for these wonderful creatures that enchant us and brighten our lives. God, bless the cats everywhere. Amen.

Rev. Lauren McLaughlin

DIVINE BLESSING

Almighty Lord, giver of all blessings,
you feed our bodies and clothe our souls
in a garment of peace.
You watch over us as a mother cat
draws her kittens to their first drink.
You created the beauty above and around us.
And in every fern and wolf,
every river birch and lark,
your spirit sings.
You have opened our eyes in your presence,
bathing us with the knowledge that you
are the bringer of all blessings.

Lynn L. Caruso, inspired by the Atharva Veda,
c. 1500 BCE

Lovers put themselves into the selves of their loved ones, seeking identity; the cat never does. Mystics try to lose themselves in union with their gods; the cat never does.... Navajo women, when they weave blankets, go so completely into the blanket while they are working on it, that they always leave a path in the weaving that comes out at the last corner for their souls to get out of the blanket; otherwise they would be imprisoned in it. The cat never does things like this!

So every one really centers his self somewhere outside of himself; every one gets out of his body. The cat never does. Every one has a false center. Only the cat—the feline—has a true centredness inside himself.

Carl Van Vechten

THE CAT AND THE MOON

The cat went here and there
And the moon spun round like a top,
And the nearest kin of the moon
The creeping cat looked up.
Black Minnaloushe stared at the moon,
For wander and wail as he would
The pure cold light in the sky
Troubled his animal blood.
Minnaloushe runs in the grass
Lifting his delicate feet.
Do you dance, Minnaloushe, do you dance?
When two close kindred meet
What better than call a dance,
Maybe the moon may learn,
Tired of that courtly fashion,
A new dance turn.
Minnaloushe creeps through the grass
From moonlit place to place,
The sacred moon overhead
Has taken a new phase.
Does Minnaloushe know that his pupils
Will pass from change to change,
And that from round to crescent,
From crescent to round they range?
Minnaloushe creeps through the grass

Alone, important and wise,
And lifts to the changing moon
His changing eyes.

William Butler Yeats

Animals are not full of cant like humans when it comes to experiencing the divine. They simply are.

Walt Whitman

~

I love cats because I enjoy my home; and little by little, they become its visible soul.

Jean Cocteau

~

There are two means of refuge from the miseries of life: music and cats.

Albert Schweitzer

EXCERPT FROM *JUBILATE AGNO*

For I will consider my Cat Jeoffry.

For he is the servant of the Living God duly and daily serving him.

For at the first glance of the glory of God in the East he worships in his way.

For this is done by wreathing his body seven times round with elegant quickness.

For then he leaps up to catch the musk, which is the blessing of God upon his prayer.

For he rolls upon prank to work it in.

For having done duty and received blessing he begins to consider himself.

For this he performs in ten degrees.

For first he looks upon his forepaws to see if they are clean.

For secondly he kicks up behind to clear away there.

For thirdly he works it upon stretch with the forepaws extended.

For fourthly he sharpens his paws by wood.

For fifthly he washes himself.

For sixthly he rolls upon wash.

For seventhly he fleas himself, that he may not be interrupted upon the beat.

For eighthly he rubs himself against a post.

For ninthly he looks up for his instructions.

For tenthly he goes in quest of food.

For having consider'd God and himself he will consider his neighbour.

For if he meets another cat he will kiss her in kindness.

...

For he keeps the Lord's watch in the night against the adversary.

For he counteracts the powers of darkness by his electrical skin and glaring eyes.

For he counteracts the Devil, who is death, by brisking about the life.

...

For he purrs in thankfulness, when God tells him he's a good Cat.

For he is an instrument for the children to learn benevolence upon.

For every house is incomplete without him and a blessing is lacking in the spirit.

...

For he is a mixture of gravity and waggery.

For he knows that God is his Saviour.

For there is nothing sweeter than his peace when at rest.

For there is nothing brisker than his life when in motion.

...

For God has blessed him in the variety of his
  movements.
For, tho he cannot fly, he is an excellent
  clamberer.
For his motions upon the face of the earth are
  more than any other quadruped.
For he can tread to all the measures upon the
  music.
For he can swim for life.
For he can creep.

Christopher Smart

3 *Blessings for Other Companion Animals*

ST. FRANCIS AND THE SOW

The bud
stands for all things,
even for those things that don't flower,
for everything flowers, from within, of self-blessing;
though sometimes it is necessary
to reteach a thing its loveliness,
to put a hand on its brow
of the flower
and retell it in words and in touch
it is lovely
until it flowers again from within, of self-blessing;
as St. Francis
put his hand on the creased forehead
of the sow, and told her in words and in touch
blessings of earth on the sow, and the sow
began remembering all down her thick length,
from the earthen snout all the way
through the fodder and slops to the spiritual curl of
    the tail,

from the hard spininess spiked out from the spine
down through the great broken heart
to the blue milken dreaminess spurting and
    shuddering
from the fourteen teats into the fourteen mouths
        sucking
    and blowing beneath them:
the long, perfect loveliness of sow.

Galway Kinnell

Be thankful to the horse that has carried you
    safely and swiftly to the end of your journey.
Be thankful to the bullock that has carried your
    burden.
Be thankful to the cow that gives her milk freely.

Buddhist prayer

~

God took a handful of southerly wind, blew
His breath over it and created the horse.

Bedouin legend

THE GIFT

When I offer the pear
and he takes it
with first
whiskered lips and then teeth
and soon it is no longer
fruit but goes into
betweenness and vanishment,
turning to pastern
and tail and good wall of the hoof
and small tithing of gold
for the pasture or fire roads —
for always where
there is offering, there is return;
when this happens
and he is careful even in greed,
even in the undignity
of his foolish — no, it must be
named true — his entirely goofy adoration
and long-tongued worship of pears;
when he knows what is pear,
what is hand, when he looks
in my face as he chews and the crush
slobbers out and foams bright as spent happiness
onto my foot, onto my sleeve,

as I bend then to lift him a wedge he has
    dropped;
when the heron holds steady in
contemplation not a few feet away,
its eyes once again closed like two stones
that have rested an hour in the sun
and gone back into leaning and dimness,
a little heat kept in them still;
when the late cars sweep by without pause,
without seeing, yet store in the
blue-shadowed beakers their own mild exchanges
of hidden, unwordable sweetness —
then the world is that actress from a Sanskrit
    poem,
whose greatness was showing two feelings at
    once:
The mercies are boundless. Every country is
    death's.

Jane Hirshfield

Encompass each goat, sheep and lamb,
Each cow and horse and store,
Surround Thou the flocks and herds,
And tend them to a kindly fold,
Tend them to a kindly fold.

Celtic blessing

~

And O my people!
This she-camel of Allah is
A symbol to you:
Leave her to feed
On Allah's (free) earth,
And inflict no harm
On her.

Qur'an 11:64

TAPESTRY OF ONENESS

An elegy for my sheep

Thank you for seven years of wool
that I have washed and rinsed by hand;
spun into yarn, and dyed with indigo,
sage and madder root.

Thank you for seven years of yarn,
which in your memory, I have woven
into stories about Celtic lands, desert journeys,
and the mud homes of ancient Basra.

Hands deep in your fleece, I am reminded
of what Apostle Philip said, "God is a dyer,
and a genuine dye becomes one with the matter
it permeates, giving it the color of immortality."

Because of your wool
my tapestries exude Spirit.
Your lanolin still glistens
in the weave of my work
as if something holy lives in it.

                              Meghan Nuttall Sayres

AT MILKING TIME

Bless, O God, my little cow,
Bless, O God, my desire;
Bless Thou my partnership
And the milking of my hands, O God
Bless, O God, each teat,
Bless, O God, each finger;
Bless Thou each drop
That goes into my pitcher, O God!

Gaelic blessing

All cattle rest upon their pasturage,
The trees and the plants flourish,
The birds flutter in their marshes,
Their wings are uplifted in adoration to thee.
All the sheep dance upon their feet,
All winged things fly,
They live when thou hast shone upon them.

Pharaoh Akhenaton, from the hymn
to the sun god Aton

While some of Your creatures live pampered lives, many others support our planet with loving service. Those animals which are herders and beasts of burden give their energy each day to enhance the lives of others. Please, God, make their working experience a happy one. Place into the hearts of their owners and keepers an awareness of the importance of these loyal and dedicated workers to their quality of life. Remind them to treat their animals lovingly and fairly and to praise their animals at the end of each working day for the work that they have done. Thank You, God, for Your special attention to the working animals in our world. Amen.

Rev. Lauren McLaughlin

PIED BEAUTY

Glory be to God for dappled things—
    For skies of couple-colour as a brinded cow;
      For rose-moles all in stipple upon trout
        that swim;
Fresh-firecoal chestnut-falls; finches' wings;
    Landscape plotted and pieced—fold, fallow,
      and plough;
      And all trades, their gear and tackle and
      trim.
All things counter, original, spare, strange;
    Whatever is fickle, freckled (who knows
        how?)
      With swift, slow; sweet, sour; adazzle,
      dim;
He fathers-forth whose beauty is past change:
    Praise Him.

Gerard Manley Hopkins

All spiritual life meets us within natural life.
Reverence for life, therefore, is applied to natural life and spiritual life alike. In the parable
of Jesus, the shepherd saves not merely the
soul of the lost sheep but the whole animal.
The stronger the reverence for natural life, the
stronger grows also that for spiritual life.

Albert Schweitzer

~

For those, O Lord, the humble beasts, that
bear with us the burden and heat of the day,
and offer their guileless lives for the well-being
of their countries: we supplicate Thy tenderness of heart, for Thou hast promised to save
both man and beast, and great is Thy loving
kindness, O Master, Saviour of the world.

Eastern Orthodox prayer

We were the family who couldn't keep pets, until Tuffy. This box turtle who had already survived two families of boys only needed some limp lettuce and a bowl of water every night. Still we managed to neglect him until one sunny June day when he disappeared into the bushes after a backyard bath. Drying Conor and Megan's tears, I assured them that Tuffy wasn't like our other pets. That he had just wandered off and would soon return home. But days dragged into weeks, and we feared Tuffy would die in the cold of an Alaskan winter. One fall day I walked out to get our newspaper, and tripped over a huge lump. "Tuffy," I screamed, snatching him up, and running inside.

"Oh, Mom," Megan said, holding the turtle close, "he came home, just like you promised."

And that night I prayed:

Dear Creator, thank you, for bringing Tuffy back home to us and joy back to our family. Just as we had given up hope, our pet turtle appeared, giving us another chance. So too you love us, no matter how much we neglect you. Like Tuffy, you may sometimes seem far away because we can't see or hear you. But all summer you were both nearby.

Oh, God of Second Chances, help us learn to take better care of Tuffy, so that he can live a long life. May our dear turtle remind us every day of your love and the chance to start anew. Amen.

Claire Rudolf Murphy

THE MAGNIFICENT BULL

My bull is white like the silver fish in the river,
White like the shimmering crane bird on the river
    bank,
White like fresh milk!
His roar is like the thunder to the Turkish
    cannon on the steep shore.
My bull is dark like the raincloud in the storm.
He is like summer and winter.
Half of him is dark like the storm cloud
Half of him is light like sunshine.
His back shines like the morning star.
His brow is red like the beak of the hornbill.
His forehead is like a flag, calling the people from
    a distance.
He resembles the rainbow.
I will water him at the river,
With my spear I shall drive my enemies.
Let them water their herds at the well;
The river belongs to me and my bull.
Drink, my bull, from the river; I am here to
    guard you with my spear.

Traditional song of the Dinka tribe, Africa

Part 2

Blessings for Wild Animals

Years ago while hiking along a remote stretch of the Pacific Coast, I encountered several ancient petroglyphs of the Makah Indians. One carving of an orca whale and two lyrical human faces reflected a time when the spiritual relationship between humans and wild animals was the mystical essence of life. Similar carvings and cave paintings can be found throughout the world and demonstrate the universality of such ancient connections, which extended beyond just the conquest of the hunt.

Animals and humans alike are formed from the same Creator's breath. We are radically connected to the wild. Naturalist John Muir questions why humans would consider themselves more valued than any other creature that makes up the whole of creation. "The universe would be incomplete without man," he writes, "but it would also be incomplete without the smallest transmicroscopic creature."

This section is divided into three chapters: "Animals of the Land," "Animals of the Sky," and "Animals of the Stream and Sea." In each, we find a collection of voices representing a wide variety of faith traditions, yet many of the poems, prayers, and blessings in this section share a similar language of respect. Regardless of how we personally experience it, the wildness of creation is something we all have in common.

We see striking parallels between the sacred texts of several faiths when exploring their Creator's compassion for birds. In passages from both the Bible and the Qur'an we are told to look at the birds of the air and reflect on the fact that "none can uphold them except (Allah) Most Gracious" (Qur'an 67:19) and "your heavenly Father feeds them" (Matt. 6:26). The Bhagavad Gita states beautifully that not only will God care for the birds, but that in fact *God is* the "winged one who carrieth immortality in his beak" (10.30).

There are numerous accounts of St. Francis of Assisi addressing birds and other animals as brothers and sisters. He clearly considered them to be members of the same family of creation. Throughout the pages of this book, you will find Native American writings exploring a similar kinship with the natural world. These writers share a reverence for Mother Earth and all her inhabitants and often address their Creator as "Grandfather." As they honor this familial bond, blessing creation becomes a natural consequence of living for many Native Americans. And as with any family, the way in which members interact contributes to the health of the whole.

We have much to learn from the wisdom of Native American traditions. With no formal word for "religion" in most Native American languages, life itself becomes a ceremony of religious practice.

Recently I returned to that same coast where I had first encountered the ancient whale petroglyphs. While hiking with my infant son in the San Juan Islands, we suddenly found ourselves just yards from a pod of orca whales. I have had few such sacred moments in life — what greater evidence could there be for the existence of a Creator than to witness the breach of an orca whale? Although we remained on the shore, a part of me did not. I felt a spiritual connection that arose from being *truly present* in the wild that few words could capture. It was a place where "in the sea, in the salt / ... God is also love, but without words," as D. H. Lawrence writes. Perhaps our ancestors once possessed the language to describe this spiritual connection, for they lived in intimate relationship with the wild, and perhaps it is a language we can strive to reclaim. It is my hope that in bringing you a variety of spiritual voices, you too may be drawn into that wild space, and find a common language with which to bless and honor all creatures.

4 Animals of the Land

THE PEACEABLE KINGDOM

The wolf also shall live with the lamb,
And the leopard shall lie down with the kid,
the calf and the lion and the fatling together,
and a little child shall lead them.

The cow and the bear shall graze,
their young shall lie down together;
And the lion shall eat straw like the ox.
…
They will not hurt or destroy
on all my whole mountain;
for the earth will be full of the knowledge
of the Lord
as the waters cover the sea.

Isaiah 11:6–7, 9

Should we pray aloud unto God? Pray unto Him in any way you like. He is sure to hear you, for He can hear even the footfall of an ant.

Sri Ramakrishna

~

The Mullah cries aloud to Him: and why? Is your Lord deaf? The subtle anklets that ring on the feet of an insect when it moves are heard of Him.

Kabir

~

Spider, your threads are well stretched
Wily hunter, your nets are well woven
Spider, you are assured of abundant food
Forest, be propitious
May my hunt be joyous as spider's!

Pygmy blessing

The snail does the Holy
   Will of God slowly.

               G. K. Chesterton

~

the voice that makes the land lovely
again and again it sounds
among the dark clouds
the thunder's voice
the voice above
the voice that makes the land lovely

the voice that makes the land lovely
the voice below
the voice of the grasshopper
among the little plants
again and again it sounds
the voice that makes the land lovely

       Navajo song from "The Mountain Chant"

I believe a leaf of grass is no less
    than the journey-work of the stars,
And the pismire is equally perfect, and a grain of
      sand, and
    the egg of the wren,
And the tree-toad is a chef-d'ouvre for the
      highest,
And the running blackberry would adorn
    the parlors of heaven.
And the narrowest hinge in my hand
    puts to scorn all machinery,
And the cow crunching with depressed head
    surpasses any statue,
And a mouse is miracle enough
    to stagger sextillions of infidels!

Walt Whitman

May our earth mother
be still in the wash of new snow.
May the red cedars shed their skins
and huddle in the chill.
May field mice gather leaves of gold and brown
and build their beds below the winter frost.

So that all may find comfort
in the earth's womb,
I gather sticks,
I fan the spark,
I send my prayer—
living in the flame.

Lynn L. Caruso, inspired by a Zuni prayer

THE BUDDHA SAYS

Know ye the grasses and the trees ... Then know ye the worms, and the moths, and the different sort of ants ... Know ye also the four-footed animals small and great ... the serpents ... the fish which range in the water ... the birds that are borne along on wings and move through the air ... Know ye the marks that constitute species are theirs, and their species are manifold.

Sutta-Nipata III

This lengthy passage is abbreviated. In the actual text, the ellipses replace the Buddha's teaching that for each type of creature, "Know ye the marks that constitute species are theirs, and their species are manifold."

How wonderful, O Lord, are the works of your
    hands!
The sun and the stars, the valleys and hills,
The rivers and lakes all disclose Your presence.
The roaring breakers of the sea tell of Your
    awesome might;
The beasts of the field and the birds of the air
Bespeak Your wondrous will.

In your goodness You have made us able to hear
The music of the world....
A divine voice sings through all creation.

                         Jewish prayer

Behold! In the creation
Of the heavens and the earth;
In the alternation of the Night and the Day;
…
In the beasts of all kinds
That He scatters
Through the earth;
In the change of the winds,
And the clouds which they
Trail like their slaves
Between the sky and the earth —
(Here) indeed are Signs
For a people that are wise.

Qur'an 2:164

PRAYER ON BOUGACHELLA PEAK

Olympic Rainforest 1991

Creator of the highest places,
of the river and blue glacier
that led me here.
Of the horned owl in the hemlock —
a purse of feathers snapped shut
and waiting out the day.

Creator of the alpine lake,
of the wind and stones
that call this forest home.
Of the black bear wading at the shore —
baptized in the setting sun.

Creator of this mountain peak,
of the crown of clouds
that veil the valley far below.
Of the buck that stands beside my tent —
watching me and waiting.

I open my mouth to speak, to praise,
to offer something to your hymn.
But all is silent.
Night wheels in a cart of plums,
the buck steps up and over the cliff's edge.

Clouds shatter,
Amen.
The sun falls through
and Amen.

Lynn L. Caruso

And to all the animals on land, to all the birds of the sky, and to everything that creeps on earth, in which there is the breath of life, [I give] all the green plants for food. And it was so. And God saw all that He had made, and found it very good. And there was evening and there was morning, the sixth day.

Genesis 1:30–31

~

We give you thanks, most gracious God, for the beauty of earth and sky and sea, ... for the songs of birds and the loveliness of flowers, and for the wonder of your animal kingdom. We praise you for these good gifts and pray that we may safeguard them for posterity.... Amen.

Bishop Mark S. Sisk

God, bless the animals ... and especially the elephants—the world's largest living land mammals. Native to India and Africa, elephants are now found on all the continents of the planet, serving as work animals and animals used for show and entertainment. Within their natural herds, God, You created elephants to demonstrate great affection for and loyalty to one another. Show us how to emulate those traits in our care for these giants, today. Send to them, wherever they are, those souls who will treat them with kindness and affection and appreciate their innate loyalty. Grant each elephant in Your loving care, God, a safe place to live, a long and comfortable life and gentle caretakers. Thank You, God, for bringing our attention to these marvelous animals today. Bless the elephants—everywhere. Amen.

Rev. Lauren McLaughlin

I am the male puma who lies upon the earth.
The knowledge of my courage has spread across
    the land.
The god of day sits in the heavens.
I sit close to the god of day.

Osage ceremonial song

~

Come back, O Tigers! to the woods again,
and let it not be leveled with the plain.
For without you, the axe will lay it low.
You, without it, forever homeless go.

Buddhist saying

5 Animals of the Sky

FOGBANK, *ELLIOTT BAY*

black flutter of cormorants
scything the surface

early light catches
wavetops in the low chop

now
the whole harbor has wings

Alicia Hokanson

~

The Magpie! The Magpie! Here underneath
In the white of his wings are the footsteps of
　　　morning.
It dawns! It dawns!

Navajo song

Do they not observe
The birds above them,
Spreading their wings
And folding them in?
None can uphold them
Except (Allah) Most Gracious:
Truly it is He
That watches over all things.

Qur'an 67:19

Look at the birds of the air; they neither sow
nor reap nor gather into barns, and yet your
heavenly Father feeds them.

Matthew 6:26

Birds make great sky-circles
of their freedom.
How do they learn it?

They fall, and falling,
they're given wings.

Rumi

~

Of children I am the childhood, and Time am
I in numbers; of beasts, I am the lord of beasts,
and among birds, I am that winged one who
carrieth immortality in his beak.

Bhagavad Gita 10.30

SNOWY HERON

What lifts the heron leaning on the air
I praise without a name. A crouch, a flare,
a long stroke through the cumulus of trees,
a shaped thought at the sky—then gone. O rare!
Saint Francis, being happiest on his knees,
would have cried *Father!* Cry anything you please.
But praise! By any name or none. But praise
the white original burst that lights
the heron on his two soft kissing kites.
When saints praise heaven lit by doves and rays,
I sit by pond scums till the air recites
its heron back. And doubt all else. But praise.

John Ciardi

My brothers, birds, you should praise your Creator very much and always love him; he gave you feathers to clothe you, wings so that you can fly, and whatever else was necessary for you. God made you noble among his creatures, and he gave you a home in the purity of the air; though you neither sow nor reap, he nevertheless protects and governs you without any solicitude on your part.

St. Francis of Assisi, from
"The Sermon to the Birds"

A HEALTH TO THE BIRDS

Here's a health to the birds one and all!
A health to the birds great and small!
The birds that from hill and hedge call,
Through the highlands and islands of grey
    Donegal —
Here's a health to them,
    Health to them,
        Health to them all!
  ...
Here's a health to the blackbird!
A health to the blackbird who hides in the
        bush,
In the glen, far from men, where the dark rivers
    rush,
And rolls a full soul in the round notes that
        gush
From his silver-toned throat at dawning's first
    flush —
        A health to the blackbird!
  ...
Here's a health to the birds one and all!
A health to the birds great and small!
The birds that from hill and hedge call,
Through the highlands and islands of grey
    Donegal —

Here's a health to them,
 Health to them,
  Health to them all!

Seumas MacManus

Everything the Power of the World does is done
in a circle.
The sky is round, and I have heard that the earth
is round
like a ball, and so are all the stars. The wind, in
its greatest
power, whirls. Birds make their nests in circles,
for theirs is
the same religion as ours. The sun comes forth
and goes down
again in a circle. The moon does the same, and
both are round.

Even the seasons form a great circle in their
changing, and always come back again to
where they were. The life of a man is a circle
from childhood to childhood, and so it is in
everything where power moves.

Black Elk

THE BIRD

Though the evening comes with slow steps and
    has signaled for all songs to cease;
Though your companions have gone to their rest
    and you are tired;
Though fear broods in the dark and the face of
    the sky is veiled;
Yet, bird, O my bird, listen to me, do not close
    your wings.

The lone night lies along your path, the dawn
    sleeps behind the shadowy hills.
The stars hold their breath counting the hours,
    the feeble moon swims the deep night.
Bird, O my bird, listen to me, do not close your
    wings.

There is no hope, no fear for you.
There is no word, no whisper, no cry.
There is no home, no bed of rest.
There is only your own pair of wings and the
    pathless sky,
Bird, O my bird, listen to me, do not close your
    wings.

Rabindranath Tagore

FIRE-FLY SONG

Flitting white-fire insects!
Wandering small-fire beasts!
Wave little stars about my bed!
Weave little stars into my sleep!
Come, little dancing white-fire bug,
Come, little flitting white-fire beast!
Light me with your white-flame magic,
Your little star-torch.

Ojibwa song

On the temple's great
Bronze bell,
A butterfly sleeps
In the noon sun.

Buson

~

A snowy mountain
Echoes in the
Jeweled eyes
Of a dragonfly.

Issa

6　Animals of the Stream and Sea

THE WAY TO OPEN

Off Lopez Island on Puget Sound
two otters rolled and dove
for abalone.
They pried free
those muscles of suction
from boulders beneath the waves.

I lifted one shell
discarded on the rocky shore.
Far back within its reaches
pearly mother
light cast back my shadow
and the sky behind me gathered hue.

The otters, all whiskers and dog-jowls,
watched over their shoulders
and swam away.
I wanted to slide
beside them through the surf
and recover something I'd mislaid.

There is this rich
food inside us no one knows
the way to open.

Paul Lindholdt

SEAL LULLABY

Oh! hush thee, my baby, the night is behind us,
    And black are the waters that sparkled so
        green.
The moon o'er the combers, looks downward to
        find us
    At rest in the hollows that rustle between.
Where billow meets billow, there soft be thy
        pillow;
    Ah, weary wee flipperling, curl at thy ease!
The storm shall not wake thee, nor shark
        overtake thee,
    Asleep in the arms of the slow-swinging seas.

Rudyard Kipling

You make springs gush forth in the valleys;
they flow between the hills,
giving drink to every wild animal;
the wild asses quench their thirst.
By the streams the birds of the air have their
    habitation;
they sing among the branches.
From your lofty abode you water the mountains;
the earth is satisfied with the fruit of your work.
You cause the grass to grow for the cattle,
    …
the stork has its home in the fir trees.
The high mountains are for the wild goats;
the rocks are a refuge for the coneys.
You have made the moon to mark the seasons;
the sun knows its time for setting.
You make darkness, and it is night,
when all the animals of the forest come creeping
    out.
The young lions roar for their prey,
seeking their food from God.
When the sun rises, they withdraw
and lie down in their dens.
    …
O Lord, how manifold are your works!
In wisdom you have made them all;
the earth is full of your creatures.

Yonder is the sea, great and wide,
creeping things innumerable are there,
living things both small and great.

Psalm 104:10–14, 17–22, 24–25

You, O God, sustain all, do good to all, and provide food for all the creatures you have created. Blessed are you, O Lord, who sustains all.

Traditional Hebrew prayer

~

Whenever a fish was caught and Francis was nearby, he would return the fish to the water, warning it not to be caught again. On several occasions the fish would linger awhile near the boat, listening to Francis preach, until he gave them permission to leave. Then they would swim off. In every work of art, as St. Francis called all creation, he would praise the artist, our loving Creator.

John Bookser Feister

May there be peace in the waters,
    Where sharks and minnows swim among the
        weeds.
May there be peace on earth,
    Where rabbits share the cool of their burrows
        with roots and seeds.
May there be peace in the skies,
    Where bees and monarchs sip the sun's sweet
        cup.

May the earth sing with the hymn of all creation.

Lynn L. Caruso

They say the sea is cold, but the sea contains
the hottest blood of all, and the wildest, the most
     urgent.

All the whales in the wider deeps, hot are they, as
     they urge
on and on, and dive beneath the icebergs.
The right whales, the sperm-whales, the hammer-
     heads, the killers
there they blow, there they blow, hot wild white
          breath out of
     the sea!

And they rock, and they rock, through the
          sensual ageless ages
on the depths of the seven seas,
and through the salt they reel with drunk delight
and in the tropics tremble they with love
and roll with massive, strong desire, like gods.
     …
And enormous mother whales lie dreaming
          suckling their whale-
     tender young
and dreaming with strange whale eyes wide open
          in the waters of
     the beginning and the end.

And bull-whales gather their women and whale-
    calves in a ring
when danger threatens, on the surface of the
    ceaseless flood
and range themselves like great fierce Seraphim
    facing the threat
encircling their huddled monsters of love.
And all this happens in the sea, in the salt
where God is also love, but without words:
and Aphrodite is the wife of whales
most happy, happy she!

        D. H. Lawrence, from "Whales Weep Not"

SONG OF SALMON

Many are running into shore,
Others with me,
True salmon gone the long way.

For they are running ashore
To you, stout pole
At the center of the heavens.

Dancing from the far world to shore
With me now,
True salmon gone the long way,

Know that they run dancing
To you, right side
Of the face of the heavens.

Towering beyond, and reaching past,
And outshining all,
True salmon gone the long way.

Paul Lindholdt, translated from the Kwakiutl

Ah, the pickerel of Walden! ... They are not green like the pines, nor gray like the stones, nor blue like the sky; but they have, to my eyes, if possible, yet rarer colors, like flowers and precious stones, as if they were the pearls, the animalized nuclei or crystals of the Walden water. They, of course, are Walden all over and all through; are themselves small Waldens in the animal kingdom, Waldenses. It is surprising that they are caught here — that in this deep and capacious spring, far beneath the rattling teams and chaises and tinkling sleighs that travel the Walden road, this great gold and emerald fish swims. I never chanced to see its kind in any market; it would be the cynosure of all eyes there. Easily, with a few convulsive quirks, they give up their watery ghosts, like a mortal translated before his time to the thin air of heaven.

Henry David Thoreau, from "Winter Animals,"
in Walden

The insect in the plant, the moth which spends its
brief hours of existence hovering about the candle's
flame—nay, the life which inhabits a drop of water,
is as much an object of God's special providence as
the mightiest monarch on his throne.

Henry Bergh

~

Beyond the temple
And the garden lanterns,
Swans
Afloat and asleep …

Shiki

~

Frog-school competing
With lark-school
Softly at dusk
In the art of song …

Shiki

~

In a moonlit night on a spring day,
The croak of a frog
Pierces through the whole cosmos
Turning it into
A single family.

Chang Chiu-Ch'eng

Part 3

Blessings from Animals

$\mathcal{I}$n the midst of researching this book, my three young sons were busy raising painted lady caterpillars. Immersed in my work, I hardly noticed the caterpillars' metamorphosis until the day my six-year-old announced they were ready to be released. No sooner did we open the door to the habitat than one butterfly burst forth and disappeared high above our house. As Rabindranath Tagore writes, "The butterfly counts not months but moments, and has time enough."

Many of the poems, prayers, and blessings in this section can serve as metaphors for our own spiritual journeys. As with my sons' butterflies, animals teach us to be present in the moment—to "live mindfully." This sentiment is invoked by many Buddhist writers, and Bashō illustrates this beautifully with his haiku about the life of the cicada. When animals are viewed as metaphors for our own spiritual lives, when we approach them expecting to learn something about ourselves or our world, we open ourselves up to blessings of insight.

Eagle Chief Letakos-Lesa of the Pawnees once said, "In the beginning of all things, wisdom and knowledge were with the animals, for Tirawa, the One Above, did not speak directly to man." The Native American practice of a vision quest sends individuals in search of an animal that will become their personal totem (symbolic animal). The individual respects and honors the animal's spirit, and in turn, the revealed totem serves as a spiritual guide. Similarly, the Bible tells us to "ask the animals, and they will teach you; the birds of the air, and they will tell you" (Job 12:7–10). By entering into the company of animals, the writers on these pages have discovered spiritual insights into birth, life, and death.

In observing the way animals simply live their lives, we discover models for our own. In the wild, we find a deep respect and loyalty inherent in a pack of wolves and a passion for life in the play of dolphins. And with our own companion animals, we are often the recipients of unconditional love, devoted trust, and forgiveness— blessings found in only the closest relationships.

Many of the holy texts not only portray animals as evidence of a Creator but tell of animals offering praise to their Creator, as echoed in the words of the Qur'an: "Each one knows its own (mode of) prayer and praise" (24:41). Once again, animals serve as examples—their very lives are an act of praise.

Traditional Native American teachings emphasize the interconnectedness of the earth and her inhabitants. All creation is considered sacred. Harming creation will result in the return of harm. Honoring or blessing creation will bring a return of blessing. I think children are more open to this possibility for blessing, perhaps because they are more open to the beauty around them and the inherent goodness of the world. Children approach life expecting to find the sacred, expecting to be blessed, expecting that what they touch will in some way touch them. And I think this connection is something we risk losing over time. When my son suddenly appeared beside my desk and announced he had a poem for my book—and then spoke the words exactly as they appear here on page 135—I was struck by his connection to the natural world. And I realized that I was missing something, as I sat inside at my desk while he turned rocks in the garden, searching for worms, expecting life below the surface.

If we view our lives as interconnected with animals and the natural world, "We are," as Joy Harjo of the Muskogee tribe writes, "truly blessed because we / were born, and die soon within a / true circle of motion / like eagle rounding out the morning / inside us." Recognizing our connection to all creation, we feel a true sense of completion, and we open ourselves to the possibility for blessings in all passages of life.

That spring day when my sons released their butterflies, they were clearly blessed by the chance to witness the unfolding of creation. I, too, felt blessed, certainly by the insect's beauty, but also by the insights gained. As I watched my son's small fingers open the butterfly's door, I was reminded of Tagore's words and could not help but reflect on the brevity of childhood. Even though my teacher was two inches long and silent, that fragile insect spoke eloquently of being present in the moment. And in spite of looming deadlines, I took the rest of the afternoon off.

7 *Blessings for Birth*

THE CHILD IS INTRODUCED TO THE COSMOS AT BIRTH

Ho! Ye Birds, great and small, that fly in the air,
Ho! Ye Animals, great and small, that dwell in
the forest,
Ho! Ye Insects that creep among the grasses and
burrow in the ground —
I bid you hear me!
Into your midst has come a new life.
Consent ye, I implore!
Make its path smooth, that it may reach the brow
of the fourth hill.

Omaha tribal prayer

Reina's puppies were everywhere. Less than twenty-four hours old, the pups were concerned with keeping warm, finding a meal, and recharging through sleep. Reina's only concerns were keeping her pups safe, fed, and clean. She responded quickly to their calls by nuzzling them closer to her body and up to her teats. The puppies emitted little grunting noises and whines as they rooted around searching for a connection. Once established, they became quiet and relaxed. Quite simply, this is how we all start on our journey up the spiritual ladder. We seek a connection ... physical and social yearnings give way to spiritual longings and exploration.

Diana L. Guerrero, from What Animals Can Teach Us about Spirituality

Dogs, even,
    when they have pups
    to them give their love.
That is why
    mine I love.

Haïda cradle song

~

Even the sparrow finds a home,
And the swallow a nest for herself,
Where she may lay her young,
At your altars, O Lord of hosts,
My King and my God.

Psalm 84:3

THRUSHES

I think the thrush's voice is more like God's
Than many a preacher's telling of the Word;
I think the mother-thrush, who turns the sods
To find fat earth-worms for her baby bird —
And, worn by her maternal toil,
With busy eye and mild
That marks each subtle movement of the soil
Patiently tends upon her greedy child —
    She is the feathery image of that grace
    Which spends itself to feed our thankless
      race.

Evelyn Underhill

How romantic and beautiful is the life of this brave little singer on the wild mountain streams, building his round bossy nest of moss by the side of a rapid or fall, where it is sprinkled and kept fresh and green by the spray! No wonder he sings well, since all the air about him is music; every breath he draws is part of a song, and he gets his first music lessons before he is born; for the eggs vibrate in time with the tones of the waterfalls. Bird and stream are inseparable, songful and wild, gentle and strong, — the bird ever in danger in the midst of the stream's mad whirlpools, yet seemingly immortal.

John Muir, from Among the Birds
of the Yosemite

MAKING THE NEST

During the Pawnee Hako Ceremony, a circle is drawn to represent a bird's nest. Participants use their feet to draw the circle because the eagle builds its nest with its claws.

Behold where two eagles come forth!
Now they soar high over head:
See where one flies, watching, flies, guarding he
His mate who has gone to her nest, dropping
    there;
'Tis Kawas who brings there new life.
…
Within the nest the child rests its little feet,
Awaiting there the gift sent by gods above;
Descending there to him comes the promised life.

Pawnee song

Kawas is the Eagle God.

Earth our mother, breathe forth life
All night sleeping
Now awaking
In the east
Now see the dawn
Earth our mother, breathe and waken
Leaves are stirring
All things moving
New day coming
Life renewing
Eagle soaring, see the morning
See the new mysterious morning
Something marvelous and sacred
Though it happens every day
Dawn the child of God and Darkness

Pawnee prayer

ORCA BLESSING

For Eli

Blessings of quiet harbors,
the waters dark and dancing
with a field of ocean weeds.
Thin crystal skirts of jellyfish
waltzing to the music of the deep.

Blessings of startled salmon
circled 'round by the call of family.
For arias of clicks and whistles
calling one another home.
Small child in my arms,
cooing in sleep, his belly
bubbling with mother's milk.

Blessings for travel north
through current of salt waters and ferry
wakes. Past Friday Harbor and the sunken
schooner in Neah Bay, alive
with a thousand swimming eyes.

Blessing your gentle roll on roll,
your body rocking like some ancient monk,
in robe of black and mottled white.
Bowing to the sun, the stars,

to all things waiting on the shore.
My infant son swims in my arms,
dreaming of the ocean of the womb.

Blessings of salt spray,
you breech in joy, then crash again—echo of
    birth,
when your mother shook you from her swollen
body and pushed you toward your first
breath. And now, again and again, you rise,
crowning through the surface of the bay,
searching for your place
among the tides.

Your wake rolls to the shore,
breaks against the rocks, the drifted wood,
the warm sand. My son's fingers open and close
in sleep, holding some smooth piece
of all he has not seen.

Lynn L. Caruso

The Cross, the Cross
Goes deeper in than we know,
Deeper into life;
Right into the marrow
And through the bone.
Along the back of the baby tortoise
The scales are locked in an arch like a bridge,
Scale-lapping, like a lobster's sections
Or a bee's.
Then crossways down his sides
Tiger-stripes and wasp-bands.
. . .
The Lord wrote it all down on the little slate
Of the baby tortoise.
Outward and visible indication of the plan
    within,
The complex, manifold involvedness of an
    individual creature
Plotted out
On this small bird, this rudiment,
This little dome, this pediment
Of all creation,
This slow one.

D. H. Lawrence, from "Tortoise Shell"

When the frost lies white
Upon fields where travelers
Must find their shelter,
O flock of heavenly cranes,
Cover my child with your wings!

Anonymous eighth-century Japanese poet

~

Lord, purge our eyes to see
Within the seed a tree,
Within the glowing egg a bird,
Within the shroud a butterfly.
Till, taught by such we see
Beyond all creatures, thee
And hearken to thy tender word
And hear its "Fear not; it is I."

Christina Rossetti

AT THE END OF SPRING

The flower of the pear-tree gathers and turns to
    fruit;
The swallows' eggs have hatched into young
    birds.
When the Seasons' changes thus confront the
    mind
What comfort can the Doctrine of Tao give?
It will teach me to watch the days and months fly
Without grieving that Youth slips away.

Po Chü-i

8 Blessings for Life

ALTHOUGH I TRY

Although I try
to hold the single thought
of Buddha's teaching in my heart,
I cannot help but hear
the many crickets' voices calling as well.

Izumi Shikibu

~

THE OWL HOOTED

The owl was requested to do as much as he knew
    how.
He only hooted and told of the morning star,
And hooted again and told of the dawn.

Yuman and Yaqui story

But ask the animals, and they will teach you;
the birds of the air, and they will tell you;
ask the plants of the earth, and they will teach
      you;
and the fish of the sea will declare to you.
Who among all these does not know
that the hand of the Lord has done this?
In his hand is the life of every living thing
and the breath of every human being.

Job 12:7–10

~

In the beginning of all things, wisdom and knowledge were with the animals, for Tirawa, the One Above, did not speak directly to man. He sent certain animals to tell man that he showed himself through the beasts, and that from them, and from the stars and the sun and the moon, man should learn.

Eagle Chief Letakos-Lesa of the Pawnees

THE SPIDER

There is craft in this smallest insect
With strands of web spinning out his thoughts;
In his tiny body finding rest,
And with the wind lightly turning.
Before the eaves he stakes out his broad earth;
For a moment on the fence top lives through his
    life.
When you know that all beings are even thus,
You will know what creation is made of.

Sugawara no Michizane

A RABBIT NOTICED MY CONDITION

I was sad one day and went for a walk;
I sat in a field.

A rabbit noticed my condition and
came near.

It often does not take more than that to help at
    times —

to just be close to creatures who
are so full of knowing,
so full of love
that they don't
—chat,

they just gaze with
their
marvelous understanding.

St. John of the Cross

God, bless the animals. Let us remember to give thanks for all of the significant animals in our lives, past and present, and for the wonderful lessons we learn from all of Your wondrous creatures. Give us, God, the gentleness of the rabbit, the working ability of the beaver, the courage of the lion, the cunning of the fox, the bravery of the tiger and the fortitude and resiliency of the coyote. May we always have the lovely family life of the wolf, whose members care for one another with sincere devotion. Grant us the common sense of the horse, the strength of the ox and especially, God, we ask for the humor, comedy and playfulness of the sea otters and the squirrels. Bless us each with the mastery of good grooming and relaxation of our cats and with the loyalty and devotion of our dogs. Best of all, God, fill us with the sheer joy of the songbirds at dawn, heralding a new day and forgetting the past. Help us, God, to awaken to and learn from their wisdom and their sweetness, their loyalty and particularly their seeming inability to judge human beings unkindly. Amen.

Rev. Lauren McLaughlin

A BLESSING

Just off the highway to Rochester, Minnesota,
Twilight bounds softly forth on the grass
And the eyes of those two Indian ponies
Darken with kindness.
They have come gladly out of the willows
To welcome my friend and me.
We step over the barbed wire into the pasture
Where they have been grazing all day, alone.
They ripple tensely, they can hardly contain their
    happiness
That we have come.
They bow shyly as wet swans. They love each
    other.
There is no loneliness like theirs.
At home once more,
They begin munching the young tufts of spring in
    the darkness.
I would like to hold the slenderer one in my
    arms,
For she has walked over to me
And nuzzled my left hand.
She is black and white,
Her mane falls wild on her forehead,
And the light breeze moves me to caress her long
    ear

That is delicate as the skin over a girl's wrist.
Suddenly I realize
That if I stepped out of my body I would break
Into blossom.

James Arlington Wright

Sweet be the night
And sweet the dawns,
Sweet the terrestrial atmosphere;
Sweet be our Father in Heaven to us.
May the tall tree be full of sweets for us,
And full of sweets the Sun:
May our milch-kine be sweet for us.

Rig Veda 1.90.6–8

~

BUTTERFLY

O Glistening one
O Book of God
O Learned one
Open your book!

Nigerian prayer

I touch God in my song
   as the hill touches the far-away sea
     with its waterfall.

The butterfly counts not months but moments,
   and has time enough.

Rabindranath Tagore, from Fireflies

~

SUMMER IN THE METHOW

Purged from the hive,
she hovers, then
dives
into the stamen's glow

Spinning gold

A whirling dervish
on the Nootka rose
I want work like that!
Work that makes me dizzy
Makes me drunk on sweet nectar
Finds me dancing
across the plush, pink petals of all that I love.

Kathy Heffernan

BE LIKE THE BIRD

Be like the bird, who
Resting in his flight
On a twig too slight
Feels it bend beneath him,
Yet sings
Knowing he has wings.

Victor Hugo

~

Hope is the thing with feathers
    That perches in the soul,
And sings the tune without the words,
And never stops at all.

Emily Dickinson

A NOISELESS PATIENT SPIDER

A noiseless patient spider,
I marked where on a little promontory it stood
    isolated,
Marked how to explore the vacant vast
    surrounding,
It launched forth filament, filament, filament, out
    of itself,
Ever unreeling them, ever tirelessly speeding
    them.

And you O my soul where you stand,
Surrounded, detached, in measureless oceans of
    space,
Ceaselessly musing, venturing, throwing, seeking
    the spheres to connect them,
Till the bridge you will need be formed, till the
    ductile anchor hold,
Till the gossamer thread you fling catch
    somewhere, O my soul.

Walt Whitman

On this tree is a bird: it dances in the joy of life. None knows where it is: and who knows what the burden of its music may be? Where the branches throw a deep shade, there does it have its nest: and it comes in the evening and flies away in the morning, and says not a word of that which it means. None tell me of this bird that sings within me. It is neither coloured nor colourless: it has neither form nor outline: It sits in the shadow of love. It dwells within the Unattainable, the Infinite, and the Eternal; and no one marks when it comes and goes. Kabir says: "O brother Sadhu! Deep is the mystery. Let wise men seek to know where rests that bird."

Kabir

A Sadhu is a monk.

There is a hog in me ... a snout and a belly ...
a machinery for eating and grunting ... a
machinery for sleeping satisfied in the sun—I
got this too from the wilderness and the
wilderness will not let it go.

There is a fish in me ... I know I came from
saltblue water-gates ... I scurried with shoals
of herring ... I blew waterspouts with por-
poises ... before land was ... before the water
went down ... before Noah ... before the first
chapter of Genesis.

...

There is an eagle in me and a mockingbird ...
and the eagle flies among the Rocky Mountains
of my dreams and fights among the Sierra crags
of what I want ... and the mockingbird warbles
in the early forenoon before the dew is gone,
warbles in the underbrush of my Chattanoogas
of hope, gushes over the blue Ozark foothills of
my wishes—And I got the eagle and the mockingbird from the wilderness.

O, I got a zoo, I got a menagerie, inside my
ribs, under my bony head, under my red-valve
heart—and I got something else: it is a man-
child heart, a woman-child heart: it is a father

and mother and lover: it came from God-Knows-Where: it is going to God-Knows-Where — For I am the keeper of the zoo: I say yes and no: I sing and kill and work: I am a pal of the world: I came from the wilderness.

Carl Sandburg, from "Wilderness"

Thus sings the Whip-poor-will,
Follow me, follow me!
Thus speaks the Chief to him,
Yes, I will follow you!
Lo! The night darkening
Stalks through the shadow-land;
No light to beckon us
Murmurs the waterfall,
Thus sings the river-voice!
…
Follow me, follow me—
So sings the whip-poor-will!
Yes, I am following—
Thus the Chief answers him.

From the Iroquois Whip-poor-will Totem Chant

~

Catching the darkness up
I hear the Eagle-bird
Pulling the blanket back
From the east, sleeping still.
How swift he flies, bearing the sun to the
     morning;
See how he perches there on the trail of the east-sky.

Iroquois song for the Ritual of Fire and Darkness

Seest thou not that it is
Allah whose praises all beings
In the heavens and on earth
Do celebrate, and the birds
(Of the air) with wings
outspread? Each one knows
its own (mode of) prayer
And praise. And Allah
Knows well all that they do.

Qur'an 24:41–42

AN AFRICAN CANTICLE

All you tiny things, bless the Lord
Busy insects and drops of rain
Tiny colorful birds and small gazelles
Our simple lifestyle, our newborn economy
Our infant children and our new faith
All you tiny things, bless the Lord
Praise and bless him forever.
...
All you swift things, bless the Lord
A wild pig, a fleeing snake, herds of migrating
    animals
The endless running and activity of countless
    children
A lion ready to spring, girls pounding corn
Swift moving trucks stopped by rivers more swift
All you swift things, bless the Lord
Praise and bless him forever.

All you slow things, bless the Lord
Curious giraffe and thin cows searching for
    grass
The peaceful countryside and the slow pace of
    life
Spending all day making mud bricks to build a
    home

Sitting by the roadside with nowhere to go
All you slow things, bless the Lord
Praise and bless him forever.

From a prayer composed by students of
Morogoro High School, Tanzania, 1963

WHERE THE SKY OPENS

i
That day at Sea World, when Shamu
breached, an orca whose splash-down

christened the crowd, *glory*
showered everywhere: petal, fin and
   marrowbone,

as if old Adam arose, then fell
again. Naming us all.

ii
Marrowed within, might a single atom
leftover from Eden, throb on? We know

bone rejoices grit, flesh falls to ash,
spirit, some say, segues to sky …

and for every gesture ascent makes, the heart
ignites—a Roman candle, a Catherine wheel.

O to mirror gravity with grace, to leap,
to swim—fireworks between two worlds.

Laurie Klein

Linda is definitely a Zen cat. She follows the sun spots around the house. Each time she finds a satisfactory spot, she lays down, enters a state of complete relaxation, and sleeps until it is time to move to a new spot. Her sleeping posture is one of complete relaxation; there is not a tense muscle in her body. Her breathing is deep and even. She is a picture of total relaxation, totally comfortable in her body and totally comfortable in her world.

I asked Linda what I should tell you about the contemplative life, and here's what she said … "Imagine that you are in your favorite place—a place that is safe and full of love. Now find the sunny spot in that place. Walk around in the sunny spot a couple of times, while feeling the warmth on your body. Then lay down in the sunny spot. The position is not important; your body will find the natural curve for the spot. Just let yourself melt into the warmth beneath you, while absorbing the warmth all around you. Breathe deeply. Relax. Know that everything is okay at this moment, just the way it is, just the way you are. Sunny spots never stay in one place, you will have to leave it. But take with you the knowledge that you are okay, at any given moment, just the way you are."

Rev. Roberta Finkelstein, from her sermon
"The Spirituality of Cats and Dogs"

What is necessary is to be. The cat knows this. Maybe, that is why the cat has been an object of worship; maybe the ancients felt intuitively that the cat had the truth in him.

...

The cat understands pure being, which is all we need to know and which it takes a lifetime to learn. It is both subject and object. It is its own outlet and its own material.... Being its own centre, it radiates electricity in all directions.

Carl Van Vechten

PRAYER FOR RAIN

White floating clouds,
Clouds like the plains
Come and water the earth.
Sun embrace the earth
That she may be fruitful.
Moon, lion of the north,
Bear of the west,
Badger of the south,
Wolf of the east,
Eagle of the heavens,
Shrew of the earth,
…
Intercede with the cloud people for us,
That they may water the earth.

Sia tribal prayer

Stray birds of summer come to my window
to sing and fly away.
And yellow leaves of autumn,
which have no songs,
flutter and fall there with a sigh.

O troupe of little vagrants of the world,
leave your footprints in my words.
…
The fish in the water is silent,
The animal on the earth is noisy,
The bird in the air is singing.
But Man has in him
The silence of the sea,
The noise of the earth
And the music of the air.

Rabindranath Tagore

Let everything that has breath
Praise the Lord.
The donkeys stampede on their feet,
The owls hoo,
The roosters cock-a-doodle-doo
And flap their wings,
The tigers roar,
The snakes rattle,
And the ducks quack and flap.
Let everything that has breath
Talk to the Lord
And praise Him.

Isaac Caruso, age 6

9   *Blessings in Death*

A GREEN CRAB'S SHELL

Not, exactly, green:
closer to bronze
preserved in kind brine,

something retrieved
from a Greco-Roman wreck,
patinated and oddly

muscular. We cannot
know what his fantastic
legs were like—

Though evidence
suggests eight
complexly folded

scuttling works
of armament, crowned
by the foreclaws'

gesture of menace
and power. A gull's
gobbled the center,

leaving this chamber
—size of a demitasse—
open to reveal

a shocking, Giotto blue.
Though it smells
of seaweed and ruin,

this little traveling case
comes with such lavish lining!
Imagine breathing

surrounded by
the brilliant rinse
of summer's firmament.

What color is
the underside of skin?
Not so bad, to die,

if we could be opened
into *this*—
if the smallest chambers

of ourselves,
similarly,
revealed some sky.

Mark Doty

Nothing in the cry
of cicadas suggests they
are about to die.

Bashō

~

How hard it is to meet my Lord! The rain-bird
wails for thirst for the rain: almost she dies of
her longing, yet she would have none other
water than the rain. Drawn by the love of
music, the deer moves forward: she dies as she
listens to the music, yet she shrinks not in fear.

Kabir

I. THE OLD DOG SPEAKS

Little woman, I see you are sad.
You say you don't know how to mourn
for your brother.
"There's no map," you tell me.
"My mother's death, my father's, they were
a different country.
Michael was younger than I.
I am lost."

Listen.
I, too, lost a brother, younger,
beloved —
the border collie who was ten years my
    companion,
black and white to my golden,
shadow to my sun.
Not of my litter, but a brother still.

When you returned that last time without him,
you held out his collar.
I sniffed it. I smelled his sweet earthy smell. I
    looked at your face.
Turning my back, I sought out my den.
For three days I lay there, coming out only to eat
and do my business in the silent yard.
I was naked without him.

I lay still in the dark and waited, until he came to
    me.
I breathed him in:
his face, his bark,
how he sang when you dished out our chow.

I breathed in the day you first brought him home.
    It was winter,
raining for weeks.
How excited we were, sniffing and bowing. We
    ran
the back lawn into circles of mud, came crashing,
exhausted, into the kitchen,
sides heaving, tongues out, crazed
with celebration.

We ran like young wolves in those days—
ran for joy, ran after rabbits
and gibbering ground squirrels. He hated their
    taunts. Down banks,
under pines, we pursued them
drove them down to their foul, dark burrows.

I breathed in those summers we swam. I was
    born for that pool.
My brother was wary,
dancing for time on the concrete deck
until you praised me
for retrieving the float. You flung it again and he

flung himself into the deep end.
He swam to you, gasping,
the buoy tight in his mouth.

He loved praise, my brother.
He worshipped you.
I think he feared nothing. While I cowered from
    thunder
he ran cursing to meet it, driving storms from our
    valley
driving fireworks out of the sky.

For three days I curled round my memories of him
until he was part of me,
breath of my breath.
Then I got up and went on.

Lie down, little mother,
seek out your cave
away from the heat and light of the world.
Call to the brother you loved.
Lie down, take him in
then go on.

Rivage, from "The Dogs on Mourning"

THE BOUNDARY

It was my wire fence
that brought the speckled fawn down.

Dangling by her tiny, cloven hoof
she thrashed to escape.

Unlike the soft cough
of a whitetail, she shrieked in pain.

I smelled a pine-needle breeze
as I held her close, watched her

wood-nurtured eyes fix on the doe
who turned and fled

Leaving me to mother our wounds.

Meghan Nuttall Sayres

I was not aware of the moment when I first crossed the threshold of this life....

When in the morning I looked upon the light, I felt in a moment that I was no stranger in this world, that the inscrutable without name and form had taken me in its arms in the form of my own mother.

Even so, in death the same unknown will appear as ever known to me. And because I love this life, I know I shall love death as well.

The child cries out when from the right breast the mother takes it away, in the very next moment to find in the left one its consolation.

Rabindranath Tagore

Creator God,
The puppy, born with eyes sealed,
crosses the threshold into life, held in the arms
of one with his mother's form. Your arms.
He clings to the warmth of his mother's milk
and cries out in his own dark world
should he wander from her swollen belly.
Alone he is frightened, startled by his own bark.

Creator God,
Even so, in death this one shall be welcomed in
    the arms
of one with his mother's form. Your arms.
Eyes sealed as in birth. And when he finds You —
nuzzles in to the sweet cream once more,
You know him. Tell him;
I've been waiting.
And there is light of a thousand stars behind his
    eyes.

> *Lynn L. Caruso, after Rabindranath Tagore*

Rev. Roberta Finkelstein reflects on lessons learned from her dog in the wake of the 9/11 terrorist attacks.

Enthusiasm and engagement. That is the spirituality of the dog ... My dog Pepper loves me absolutely, he thinks I'm wonderful all the time, and he is absolutely enthusiastic about the world.

The word enthusiasm has an interesting root. It goes back to the Greek *en theos* — the indwelling of God. Enthusiasm is not mindless, it is a deep and abiding belief in the goodness of life. That's the spirituality of the dog — engaged with the world, out there seeing and smelling and interacting. And constantly affirming its basic goodness ...

On September 12th, when I woke up the day after, exhausted from a mostly sleepless night and wondering how I could possibly prepare for the services I had promised that evening, it was Pepper who helped me get back my perspective.

For Pepper, the morning after September 11 was a morning like any other. He charged up from his bed, headed straight for the door, wriggled in anticipation while I hooked on his leash, then charged out the door and down the porch steps. Oh, those first sniffs at the bushes! Ah, that first whiff of green grass. Always we go the first couple of houses with his nose buried in the delicious smells of the neighborhood. Then, as we approach the mini-park, he stops and looks back at me. "Isn't this great?" he asks, tail wagging. "Can you believe it's all still here?"

I don't know which was harder to believe that morning. That the Twin Towers were gone, that the seemingly impregnable Pentagon walls had been breached. Unbelievable! Or was it even more unbelievable what Pepper told me that morning. That it—the grass, the bushes, the familiar smells and stops along our regular morning route, it was all still there in all its glory.

Pepper doesn't know much about terrorism or foreign policy. But what he does know is that all that was right and wonderful and dependable about our life on September 10th is still here. He knows it because of his enthusiasm for life—his ability to embody the indwelling of goodness and rightness. He teaches me, every morning, a most important lesson: be uncomplicated, be genuine, be glad to be alive. Because (sniff) it's all still here!

Rev. Roberta Finkelstein

A GOLD CAT

I.
she slips in from the midnight yard
calling *where are you   where?*
the moon is full
then loud lapping at her water bowl

grazing your face with a furred
edge of claw
smelling sweetly of soil and air and leaf
she circles and settles

on the quilt   her ear alert
for your waking
her tongue hidden
against her saber teeth

II.
you don't know how to love
except you could
adore an orange cat
lying in a bed of sunlight

she lifts her head to look at you
all ease and acceptance
offering her white belly
she licks her paw and then your hand

her language is fur twinings
and a willfulness
that bats the pen from your fingers

her teaching:
a purring and fierce attention
a surrender
to the hand stroking

III.
she stretches her whole silk
against you under the sheet
to be held against the dark
stabs of seizure that jerk
her to confusion

the first night of them
she staggered to the bed
her place at the foot of it
where she would meld
her sleep to yours   now

she is a child   you wake to
her changes   her stiffening
and her languor
she abandons her gold will
once wiry and sure   sleeps

all night in the crook of your arm
gives herself up

to human mothering
no longer the guardian

IV.
her body has the same heft as before
—slink of heavy gold—
her coat has not lost its rippled luster
from the last time you
held her against the seizure shudder
    (snuffle of her breath coming out of it
    tongue licking quickly
    pupils wide black)

surely her soul
weighs more than this
sack of orange sinew
you tumble into the earth

tumble into the yellow clay
among the gold-footed centipedes
under the forest duff

Alicia Hokanson

Tell me, O Swan, your ancient tale.
From what land do you come, O Swan? To what
    shore will you fly?
Where would you take your rest, O Swan and
    what do you seek?

Even this morning, O Swan, awake, arise, follow
    me!
There is a land where no doubt nor sorrow have
    rule: where the terror of Death is no more.
There the woods of spring are a-bloom, and the
    fragrant scent "He is I" is borne on the wind:
There the bee of the heart is immersed, and
    desires no other joy.

      Kabir, translated by Rabindranath Tagore

O father of the sky, O mother earth,
Weave a cloak of beauty to clothe your children.
May the warp be the sparrow's silver song.
May the weft be the red fox hunting in the
     shadowed wood.
May the fringes be the streams that lead the
     salmon home.
May the border be the sky of stars, watching
beasts that wander with the moon.
Thus weave for us a cloak of beauty.
And at our journey's end, may we return to earth
clothed in your creation.
O father of the sky, O mother earth.

Tewa Pueblo prayer, adapted by Lynn L. Caruso

THE GRASSHOPPER

Wonderful that these sublime mountains are so loudly cheered and brightened by a creature so queer. Nature in him seems to be snapping her fingers in the face of all earthly dejection and melancholy with a boyish hip-hip-hurrah. How the sound is made I do not understand. When he was on the ground he made not the slightest noise, nor when he was simply flying from place to place, but only when diving in curves, the motion seeming to be required for the sound; for the more vigorous the diving the more energetic the corresponding outbursts of jolly rattling.... A fine sermon the little fellow danced for me on the Dome, a likely place to look for sermons in stones, but not for grasshopper sermons. A large and imposing pulpit for so small a preacher. No danger of weakness in the knees of the world while Nature can spring such a rattle as this ... And when at length his sun sets, I fancy he will cuddle down on the forest floor and die like the leaves and flowers, and like them leave no unsightly remains calling for burial.

John Muir

THREE BEES

I fish three bees from the pool with the skimmer
    net.
This time of year is hard on them —
cool nights and rain
and an urgency to fill the hive for those
who will emerge in Spring.
They go after the blue-flowered rosemary
that trails its fingers in the water. Maybe these
went for its reflection.

I breathe warm air against their sides: Bee CPR.
One spreads a wing, the other two wave legs.
I hold the net over clusters
of a late-blooming sweet alyssum
and bend a stem to each in turn,
allowing her to grasp
and slowly climb

I'll leave them here,
three sisters,
drying their wings in the sun.
Whether they fly again is not my call
but if they die,
it will be in a dream
scented with summer.

Rivage

I am like the quetzal bird, I am created in the house of the one and only God; I sing sweet songs among the flowers; I chant songs and rejoice in my heart. The fuming dewdrops from the flowers in the field intoxicate my soul. I grieve to myself that ever this dwelling on earth should end.

Aztec song

~

Small bird forgive me,
I'll hear the end
Of your song
In some other world.

Anonymous

Part 4

Rituals and Ceremonies

As a college student studying in Central America, I spent time in the Costa Rican cloud forest of Monteverde. Hiking beneath the thick canopy of trees, I was overwhelmed by the chorus of wild creatures, and the feeling I had entered a sacred place. Time and again I stood still on the path, listening in awe to the jubilation of a tree filled with howler monkeys, watching the slow workings of a three-toed sloth, and a resplendent quetzal burrowing a home in a dead tree. In his book *Dogmatics in Outline*, theologian Karl Barth describes creation as "grace" and charges humankind to pause in "reverence ... and gratitude." That pause in the depths of Monteverde remains with me today.

The final section of this book invites animals into our own rituals of worship. The animal blessing ceremonies begin with a multifaith service to be used in community, as well as an original Circle of Blessing ceremony. I found inspiration for this Circle of Blessing in the sacred Navajo Blessingway ceremony. Additionally, this section includes poems, prayers, and blessings for use in creating your own service.

Historically, the act of blessing animals originated at a time when humans relied on animals for their survival. Although this dependence is no longer as prevalent, such ceremonies continue throughout the world today. In Bali, Hindus honor their domestic animals with a ceremony called Tumpek Kandang. A feast is provided, prayers are offered, and the animals are blessed with a sprinkling of holy water and rice. In Germany, a "Blessing of the Horses" is celebrated, while in Malaysia, the Buddhist Sang Dewa ceremony involves blessing animals in the belief that they may be born into a higher realm. At one recent ceremony, ten thousand birds, fish, tortoises, and snails were blessed and released into their natural habitats.

Christian animal blessing ceremonies are often associated with St. Francis of Assisi, the patron saint of animals. At the conclusion of his famous "Sermon to the Birds," St. Francis turned to the animals present, "blessed them and, making the sign of the cross, gave them permission to fly off." Stories of St. Francis's concern for animals and his early blessing rituals abound, and today many churches offer animal blessing ceremonies on October 4, his feast day.

Religious worship services are often places where we celebrate the bond between Creator and created. It is fitting, then, that we acknowledge our companions in creation by inviting them into our sacred spaces. Webster's dictionary defines the act of blessing as, "To make or declare holy ... to ask divine favor for." This very act of blessing draws us closer to both Creator and created as we intercede on behalf of our companions.

As caring humans, we sometimes have to deal with the illness, loss, and parting of animal companions. Once again, using a Navajo ritual as inspiration, I have created a Circle of Healing ceremony to be used at home with a companion animal suffering illness or injury. This series of multifaith prayers aims to draw humans into the presence of their companion's suffering—intervening as compassionate stewards to a compassionate Creator.

The final "Partingway" ceremony is original and has no connection to any one faith tradition. Although we have more than 110 million domestic cats and dogs in the United States alone, the topic of bereavement is all too often considered socially unacceptable. I have created a multifaith ceremony in the hope that individuals experiencing such a loss will find words of comfort and support.

We, along with all animals, are part of the community of creation. God cares and provides for all members of this community, as promised in the Qur'an: "There is not an animal (that lives) on the earth, nor a being that flies on its wings, but (forms part of) communities like you. Nothing have we omitted from the Book, and they (all) shall be gathered to their Lord in the end" (6:38). The loss of a single member is mourned by all.

The book concludes with a benediction, exploring our interconnectedness with all of creation and charging us to be better stewards of our planet and its inhabitants. In Genesis, the Bible says that God created all creatures, declared them good, and then made humans in God's image—both a blessing and a tremendous responsibility. We are called to care for creation as our Creator would. As the first precept of Buddhism teaches, we must "preserve and cherish all life." With increasing numbers of animals endangered and extinct, and environmental destruction threatening our planet, we must ask ourselves, would our Creator still look upon the whole of creation and call it *good?*

I felt truly blessed when entering that wild temple in Costa Rica, where animals offered praise through song, and howl, and flight. It seems appropriate to return the blessing by including animals in our own rituals of worship, to pause in our regular religious services and reflect in "reverence … and gratitude" for the mystery of creation.

10   Animal Blessing Ceremonies

MULTIFAITH ANIMAL BLESSING CEREMONY

The specific content of this ceremony could easily be adapted by substituting other poems, prayers, and blessings found throughout this book.

INVITATION

Blessed are you, Lord our God,
King of the universe, who has withheld nothing
from your world, and has created therein
beautiful creatures and goodly trees
for the enjoyment of mankind.

Traditional Hebrew prayer

HYMN, OR OTHER SONG

(Refrain)
All things bright and beautiful,
All creatures great and small,
All things wise and wonderful:
The Lord God made them all.

(Verse 1)
Each little flower that opens,
Each little bird that sings,
He made their glowing colors,
He made their tiny wings.

(Refrain)

(Verse 4)
He gave us eyes to see them,
And lips that we might tell
How great is God Almighty,
Who has made all things well.

(Refrain)

> *Cecil Frances Alexander, "All Creatures Great
> and Small" (verses 1, 4)*

RESPONSIVE READING

Leader: Whatever living beings there are,
All: Either feeble or strong

Leader: Either long or great ...
**All: Either seen or which are not seen, and which
live far or near,**

Leader: Either born or seeking birth,
All: May all creatures be happy minded.

> *From the Sutta Nipata, 8:145–146*

SACRED TEXT READING

> There is not an animal
> (That lives) on the earth,
> Nor a being that flies
> On its wings, but (forms
> Part of) communities like you.
> Nothing have we omitted
> From the Book, and they (all)
> Shall be gathered to their Lord
> In the end.
>
> *Qur'an 6:38*

or

> All creatures go forth from Me and all return unto
> Me; thus rise and set my immense days and nights.
>
> *Bhagavad Gita 9.7*

MEDITATION

Blessing animals is a reminder that God is bigger than our own hearts, and that God's purposes take in all creatures. We bless them today to recognize their importance in their own right—that their being and their end is God's to give and part of God's plan. Blessing animals is a sign of humility and respect on our part, and an admission that humans aren't the centre of everything.

Moreover, the animals we bless today are our companions. They're part of our lives, they share our homes; the mammals among them may even share our joys and sorrows…. Because they're our companions, our friends, we're reminded that friends aren't there to be used; they're not part of any calculation of our own benefit. Friendship is one of life's great, unmerited gifts, and a sign of God's care for us. Friends are the tonic of life, and our animal friends are no exception. So our blessing today is also an act of love, of friendship and of thankfulness.

Rev. Dr. Scott Cowdell, from his St. Francis Day
Sermon "Animal Care and the New Creation"

PRAYER

Almighty God, Creator of heaven and earth.
With your breath you gave life to all creatures,
     and declared them good.
Keep us mindful of this first, most holy blessing
as we gather here today to offer our own
     blessings upon these —
our companion animals.

Remind us always that we were created in your
     image —
the image of a loving and compassionate God.
And in this image we are called to care for your
     creation.

Open our hearts and minds to the lessons we may
learn from our companions — To live fully in the
   present.
To love unconditionally. To face each day
   expecting joy.

Help us always to do your will on earth,
so that you may look upon our work
and declare it *good*. Amen.

Lynn L. Caruso

BLESSING OF THE ANIMALS

Animals to be blessed are brought forward at this time.

Live without fear ... your Creator loves you, made
you holy, and has always protected you. Go in peace
to follow the good road, and may God's blessing be
with you always. Amen.

Bishop Mark S. Sisk

BENEDICTION

All: Deep peace of the running wave to you.
Deep peace of the flowing air to you.
Deep peace of the quiet earth to you.
Deep peace of the shining stars to you.
Deep peace of the infinite peace to you.

Celtic blessing, attributed to Fiona McLeod

Leader: Hear me, four quarters of the world—a relative I am! Give me the strength to walk the soft earth, a relative to all that is!

Black Elk

CIRCLE OF BLESSING

The following blessing ceremony could be used at home with a single animal, or in community with others. This ceremony can be personalized by selecting other writings from the book.

REFLECTION

The Blessingway is one of the central ceremonies of the Navajo tradition and serves as a recounting of the creation story. This ritual is used for many occasions in which an individual requires special blessing.

The Navajo Blessingway involves repetition of certain blessings. It is believed that in reciting these passages, individuals recount the acts of creation and participate in the re-creation of the world. The following Circle of Blessing is preceded by a line from an actual Navajo Blessingway, then uses this same pattern for the animal blessing.

CIRCLE OF BLESSING

Leader: Listen first to the original lines from a traditional Navajo Blessingway ceremony, then join me in reading the responsive blessing.

Before Earth with small blue birds it is blessed,
　　with small blue birds before me it is blessed as I
　　　　say this.

Please place your hand upon your companion as we read this blessing together.

Leader: Upon the Earth with gentle caregivers
All: With gentle caregivers this companion is blessed.

Leader: Upon the Earth with wanderings through green spaces
All: Through green spaces this companion is blessed.

Leader: Upon the Earth with long naps in a patch of sun
All: In a patch of sun this companion is blessed.

Leader: Upon the Earth with food for the body and a home for comfort
All: With food and home this companion is blessed.

Leader: Upon the Earth with wild cousins — the wolf and lynx and hawk
All: With wild cousins this companion is blessed.

Leader: Upon the Earth with gentle caregivers
All: With gentle caregivers this companion is blessed.

If used in a service with other companion animals, participants can be encouraged to write their own verse using the same pattern. Participants could gather in a circle, each read-

ing their personal verses, until the circle of blessing has become one complete whole.

PRAYER

Eternal God, Creator of all human life, parent of the universe, help us fulfill our obligation to replenish the world. Teach us the sanctity of all life that we may truly serve as partners with you in the daily act of creation. May we learn to manifest our love for you through loving all of your creation. May we become messengers of your loving concern now and forever.

Rabbi Harold S. White

BENEDICTION

O Hidden Life, vibrant in every atom,
O Hidden Light, shining in every creature,
O Hidden Love, embracing all in Oneness,
May each who feels himself as one with Thee
Know he is therefore one with every other.

Annie Besant

Blessing of green plants, blessing of forests:
Cedar, douglas fir, swordfern, salal bush.
Blessing of fish and birds, blessing of mammals:
Salmon, eagle, cougar and mountain goat.
May all humankind likewise offer blessing ...
Bless the wisdom of the holy one above us;
Bless the truth of the holy one beneath us;
Bless the love of the holy one within us.

Chinook psalter

The Tao gives birth to all of creation.
The virtue of Tao in nature nurtures them,
and their family gives them their form.
Their environment then shapes them into
    completion.
That is why every creature honors the Tao and its
    virtue.
...
It gives them life without wanting to posses them,
and cares for them expecting nothing in return.
It is their master, but it does not seek to dominate
    them.
This is called the dark and mysterious virtue.

Lao-Tzu, from the Tao Te Ching, *translated by*
j.h. mcdonald

And God said, "Let the waters bring forth swarms of living creatures, and let birds fly above the earth across the dome of the sky." So God created the great sea monsters and every living creature that moves, of every kind, with which the waters swarm, and every winged bird of every kind. And God saw that it was good. God blessed them, saying, "Be fruitful and multiply and fill the waters in the seas, and let birds multiply on earth." And there was evening and there was morning, the fifth day.

Genesis 1:20–23

Hey-a-a-hey! Hey-a-a-hey! Hey-a-a-hey!
Hey-a-a-hey! Grandfather, Great Spirit, once
more behold me on earth and lean to hear my
feeble voice. You lived first, and you are older
than all need, older than all prayer. All things
belong to you—the two-leggeds, the four-
leggeds, the wings of the air and all green
things that live. You have set the powers of the
four quarters to cross each other. The good
road and the road of difficulties you have made
to cross; and where they cross, the place is
holy. Day in and day out, forever, you are the
life of things.

Black Elk

PRAYER TO ST. FRANCIS FOR OUR PETS

Good St. Francis, you loved all of God's
    creatures.
To you they were your brothers and sisters.
Help us to follow your example
of treating every living thing with kindness.
St. Francis, Patron Saint of animals,
watch over my pet
and keep my companion safe and healthy.
Amen.

Author unknown

Blessed are you, Lord God, maker of all living creatures. You called forth fish in the sea, birds in the air, and animals on the land. You inspired St. Francis to call all of them his brothers and sisters. We ask you to bless this pet. By the power of your love, enable it to live according to your plan. May we always praise you for all your beauty in creation. Blessed are you, Lord our God, in all your creatures! Amen.

Kevin E. Mackin, OFM

O most high, almighty, good Lord God, to thee belong praise, glory, honor, and all blessing!

Praised be my Lord God with all his creatures, and specially our brother the sun, who brings us the day and who brings us the light; fair is he and shines with a very great splendor: O Lord, he signifies to us thee!

Praised be my Lord for our sister the moon, and for the stars, which he has set clear and lovely in heaven.

Praised be my Lord for our brother the wind, and for air and cloud, and all weather by which thou upholdest life in all creatures.

St. Francis of Assisi, from
The Canticle of the Sun

Let them praise the name of the Lord,
for he commanded and they were created.
He established them forever and ever;
he fixed their bounds, which cannot be passed.

Praise the Lord from the earth,
you sea monsters and all deeps,
...
Wild animals and all cattle,
Creeping things and flying birds!
...
Let them praise the name of the Lord,
for his name alone is exalted;
his glory is above earth and heaven.

Psalm 148:5–7, 10, 13

Now, it never seems to occur to these far-seeing teachers that Nature's object in making animals and plants might possibly be first of all the happiness of each one of them, not the creation of all for the happiness of one. Why should man value himself as more than a small part of the one great unit of creation? And what creature of all that the Lord has taken the pains to make is not essential to the completeness of that unit—the cosmos? The universe would be incomplete without man; but it would also be incomplete without the smallest transmicroscopic creature that dwells beyond our conceitful eyes and knowledge.

From the dust of the earth, from the common elementary fund, the Creator has made *Homo sapiens*. From the same material He has made every other creature, however noxious and insignificant to us. They are earth-born companions and our fellow mortals.

John Muir

Apprehend God in all things,
for God is in all things.

Every single creature is full of God
and is a book about God.

Every creature is a word of God.

If I spent enough time with the tiniest creature—
Even a caterpillar—

I would never have to prepare a sermon. So full
    of God
is every creature.

Meister Eckhart

11 Partings

CIRCLE OF HEALING

REFLECTION

The Nightway is a traditional Navajo healing ritual. Individuals suffering from an illness participate in this ceremony, which lasts from sunset to sunrise over a period of nine days. The service can be traced to the eleventh century and involves songs, prayers, and sand paintings. Using the Nightway ritual as inspiration, the following Circle of Healing ceremony was created for use with animals experiencing illness or injury.

This Circle of Healing includes three days of prayers. The prayer that begins with "House made of dawn" is a traditional Navajo prayer commonly used in the Nightway ceremony. If you wish to continue the service for the full nine days, select other writings from the book for inclusion on subsequent days.

BLESSING PRAYERS

Each day, light a candle symbolizing the warmth of healing, the light of a holy presence, and the sun at dawn.

PRAYER FOR DAY 1

> May all creatures be freed from their suffering
> May all creatures be freed from their illness.
> May those in fear be comforted
> And those bound be set free.
>
> May all creatures lost in this wilderness
> they do not know
> be guarded by the love of celestials,
> and may they be led to a place
> of everlasting peace.
>
> *Buddhist Prayer, adapted by Lynn L. Caruso*

PRAYER FOR DAY 2

> Almighty God,
> Give us the wisdom to teach our children.
> May their first words be of kindness toward all
>   creatures
> and may they grow in the light of compassion.
> If an animal is sick,
> let them cure it.
> If it is hungry,

let them give it the food it desires.
If it is thirsty,
let them find cool springs for its drink.
If it is tired,
let them give it rest.

Lynn L. Caruso, inspired by Bahá'í wisdom

Prayer for Day 3

Pray these words for your companion.

House made of the dawn.
House made of evening light.
House made of the dark cloud.
...
Restore my feet for me.
Restore my legs for me.
Restore my body for me.
Restore my mind for me.
Restore my voice for me.
...
Happily I recover.
Happily my interior becomes cool.
Happily I go forth.
My interior feeling cold, may I walk.
No longer sore, may I walk.
Impervious to pain, may I walk.
With lively feelings may I walk.

As it used to be long ago, may I walk.
Happily may I walk.
Happily with abundant dark clouds, may I walk.
Happily with abundant showers, may I walk.
Happily with abundant plants, may I walk.
Happily on a trail of pollen, may I walk.
Happily may I walk.
Being as it used to be long ago, may I walk.
May it be beautiful before me.
May it be beautiful behind me.
May it be beautiful below me.
May it be beautiful above me.
May it be beautiful all around me.
In beauty it is finished.
In beauty it is finished.

Navajo blessing

BENEDICTION

The Navajo believe that *nilch'i* (holy wind) is the life-giving force behind all living things. At the end of many Navajo ceremonies, participants stand and breathe in the air at dawn, filling all with the healing, holy wind.

As you read these words, place your hand on your companion. Be aware of your companion's breathing, and close with a deep healing breath.

May pain be far away from you,
May fear be far away from you,
May there be warm winds without storm.
And may the Lord of life
Watch over you.

Lynn L. Caruso, reflection on a Hindu prayer

May all sentient beings be happy, may all sentient beings be peaceful, may all sentient beings be free from suffering.

Buddhist prayer

~

There is in the look of beasts a profound light and gentle sorrow, which fills me with such understanding that my soul opens like a hospice to all the sorrows of animals.... I seem to see a halo around the heads of these mournful creatures, a real halo, as large as the universe, placed there by God himself.

Francis Jammes, from Romance of the Rabbit

PRAYER FOR OUR ANIMAL FRIENDS

Heavenly Father, the bond we have with our friends of other species is a wonderful and special gift from You. We now ask You to grant our special animal companions your Fatherly care and healing power to take away any suffering they have. They trust in us as we trust in You. Give us, their human friends, new understanding of our responsibilities to these creatures of Yours. Our souls and theirs are on this earth together to share friendship, affection, and caring. Take our heartfelt prayers and bless these ill or suffering animals with healing Light and strength to overcome whatever weakness of body they have:

[Here mention the names of the animals needing prayer.]

Your goodness is turned upon every living thing; Your grace flows to all Your creatures; Your Light touches each of us with the reflection of Your love. Grant long and healthy lives to our special animal companions. Bless their relationships with us, and if You see fit to take them from us, help us to understand that they are not gone from us but only drawing closer to You. Grant our prayer through the intercession of good St. Francis of Assisi, who honored You through all Your creatures. Empower him to watch over our animal friends until they are safely with You in eternity, where we someday hope to join them in honoring You forever. Amen.

Gloria Pinsker

Enviable leaves,
Becoming
So beautiful
Just before falling ...

Shiki

~

Creator God,
Who names the moment of our birth and death.
Open our eyes to beauty in the midst of our loss.
And in these final days, give us patience
as our companion's steps are slowed.
Give us compassion in their care,
and give us the same selfless love
they have always shown.
Keep us present in the light of dusk.
The evening sun,
Becoming
So beautiful
Just before setting ...

Lynn L. Caruso, after the writings of Shiki

PARTINGWAY

This ceremony can be used to bring comfort to those experiencing loss of a companion animal. It is written for use with an intimate gathering of friends or family but can be easily adapted for a public service honoring the parting of more than one companion animal.

MEDITATION

> Do not stand at my grave and weep.
> I am not there.
> I do not sleep.
> I am a thousand winds that blow.
> I am the diamond glint on snow.
> I am the sunlight on ripened grain.
> I am the autumn rain.
> When you awake in the morning hush,
> I am the swift uplifting rush
> Of birds circling in flight.
> I am the stars that shine at night.
> Do not stand at my grave and weep.
> I am not there.
> I do not sleep ...

> *Author unknown*

SCRIPTURE

I said in my heart with regard to human beings that
God is testing them to show that they are but animals.
For the fate of humans and the fate of animals is the
same; as one dies, so dies the other. They all have the
same breath, and humans have no advantage over
the animals ... All go to one place; all are from the
dust, and all turn to dust again.

Ecclesiastes 3:18–21

PRAYER

Great Spirit, Great Spirit, my Grandfather, all over
the world the faces of living things are all alike. With
tenderness have these come up out of the ground.
Look upon these ... that they may face the winds and
walk the good road to the day of quiet.

Black Elk

SONG OR CHANT

Blessings of
His breath of life
His breath of warming days
His breath of spring
His breath of journeys north
His breath of geese

His breath of shifting clouds
His breath of fall
His breath of journeys south
His breath of flight.
His breath of travels home
His breath of loss.

Now into His presence He draws
your breath and you become—
His breath of morning's star
His breath of dawn.

Lynn L. Caruso, inspired by a Zuni chant

REFLECTION

The Navajo believe that all creation is given life through *nilch'i* (holy wind). We are all interconnected with this common breath, and we cannot help but notice when that wind shifts. *Nilch'i* enters a being at conception and is breathed in at all times. At death, this holy wind leaves the body.

During times of loss it seems that all is still—that the breath of joy is unmoving within us. But, as we leave this place today let us be aware of the presence of the wind—in the shifting leaves, in the bending grass, in the wings that play among the clouds. Let us always remember that with one common breath, we were all created, and in the end we shall all return in one holy inhale. Look to the gentle winds this day, and as you move forward, be ever mindful of your companion's presence.

PARTINGWAY BLESSING

Leader: As we reflect on the passing of this companion let us share communally in this responsive blessing:

Leader: Upon the Earth with gentle caregivers
All: With gentle caregivers this companion was blessed.

Leader: Upon the Earth with wanderings through green spaces
All: Through green spaces this companion was blessed.

Leader: Upon the Earth with long naps in a patch of sun
All: In a patch of sun this companion was blessed.

Leader: Beneath the Earth with the warmth of our love
All: With our love this companion is blessed.

Leader: Beneath the Earth with the turning of all things done, into seeds
All: Into seeds our companion is blessed.

Leader: Upon the Earth with the sprout of loss bloom-
ing into rose
All: Into rose our companion is blessed.

Lynn L. Caruso, inspired by a Navajo Blessingway

PRAYER

In the beginning, all creatures were hidden treas-
ures—longing to be known, and brought into being.
God then exhaled a sigh of compassion, and with that
great sigh, the world was created.

Sufi parable

Loving God,
Before _____ came to share our home, you knew
him [her], knew that he [she] longed to be brought
into this loving family.

Compassionate God,
With your breath you created the world in one sacred
exhale. And in that breath, _____ first came into
being.

Eternal God,
We return this treasured companion to you. We place
him [her] in your loving arms, where he [she] was
known even before the call of his [her] first bark

[adapt appropriately]. With your breath that created all in one compassionate exhale, draw this companion home to you in one loving inhale.

Amen.

Lynn L. Caruso

BENEDICTION

> Warm summer sun, shine kindly here;
> Warm western wind, blow softly here;
> Green sod above, lie light, lie light —
> Good-night, dear heart, good-night, good-night.

Robert Richardson's "Annette,"
adapted by Mark Twain

If it's true that we'll be made one again with all we've loved and lost in the Kingdom of God, then I can't think of one compelling theological reason why our animal friends of past times won't be with us as well.

Rev. Dr. Scott Cowdell, from his St. Francis Day Sermon "Animal Care and the New Creation"

~

O Arjuna! I am the Self, seated in the hearts of all beings; I am the beginning and the life, and I am the end of them all.

Bhagavad Gita 10.20

Arjuna was a great warrior king.

LAST WORDS FOR THE OLD CAT

I carried him, mewling in a blue satchel
across night waters to the island, to those years
of paradise: a garden walled in brambles,
rhubarb leaves he slept under, leapt from,
attacking my trowel, even his huge terror
of the beach. He'd stop on high tide logs
and call me, call me back to the cabin.

Summers on the porch under diving swallows:
with a quick swipe he snatched one out of the air,
dropped it at my feet. Brought me, too, the
    furless
rabbit pups squeaking in his jaws, chased
feral cats from the yard. And when one
    morning
he slumped at the door, eyelid raked open by a
    talon,
he wouldn't let me touch him, hid behind
shelves making a nest for his suffering.

Now again he hoards his stillness.
He does not comment
on a world beating with pain,
but hauls himself into the sun, lies at the edge
of budding currant. Evenings he pushes his back
against the heating grate. Even when he cannot

stand or drink, he arches into my hands.
Fifteen years —

I will lay him in rust-colored clay under the firs,
paws folded into the curve of his stilled body.
His speckled coat will blend with spring's
warm earth. Over him I'll stretch roots
of the new rhododendron.
I have chosen it:

One Thousand Butterflies

Alicia Hokanson

ON THE DEATH OF A CAT

Passionate Lord, by becoming one of us, you revealed your unrelenting desire to have us love you. As we were created for such love, you have made us to love your creation and through such love, such desire, learn to love you. We believe every love we have you have given us. Tuck's love of us, and our love of him, is a beacon, a participation, in your love of all your creation. We thank you, we sing your praise, for the wonderful life of this cat. His calm, his dignity, his courage, his humor, his needs, his patience, his always "being there," made us better, made our love for one another better, made us better love you. We will miss him. Help us not fear remembering him, confident that the sadness such memory brings is bounded by the joy that Tuck existed and, with us, is part of your glorious creation, a harbinger of your peaceable kingdom. Amen.

Stanley Hauerwas

BLESSING UPON THE DEATH OF A PET

Blessed are you, Creator of all the Universe
Blessed is your Spirit which brought forth birds
    of the air,
Fish of the sea and animals on land.
We gather to thank you for our beloved pet
    _____

And for all the moments of joy _____
    brought to our lives.
We remember especially …
[Each person present may share a memory, a
    special quality, or a characteristic of the pet.]
As spring follows winter, and summer follows
    spring
We know seasons of joy follow seasons of sorrow.
Bless us as we carry on the memory of
    _____'s warm touch in our lives.
The great mystery of life and death lies ever
    before us.
May we walk humbly, with reverence and gratitude.
Bless us now, as we say good-bye to _____.
[Each person may make some ritual gesture of
    parting, such as a bow, stroking the pet one
    last time, or dropping dirt into the grave].
Amen.

Mary Cronk Farrell

ELEGY ON THE DEATH OF A DOG

Quiet rest subdued with a strong hand
the poor restless dog,
and forever faithful
he lay down on the merciful
earth, his mother.
His soft eyes
he will not fasten on mine
with sadness for the lack of speech;
he will not lick my hand
nor will he lay in my lap
his fine head.
And now of what do you dream,
where has your humble spirit gone,
is there not another world
in which you live again, poor beast,
where above the skies
you frisk and gambol at my side?
...
But there, shall we not have
around our soul
the souls of the things by which it lives,
the soul of the fields,
the souls of the rocks,
the souls of the trees and the rivers,
souls of the animals?

There, in the other world,
your soul, poor dog,
will it not have to lay
in my spiritual lap its spiritual head?
The tongue of your soul, my poor friend,
will it not lick the hand of my soul?
...
I was your religion, I was your glory:
you dreamed of God in me;
my eyes were for you a window
into the other world.
What if you knew, my dog,
how sad your god is because you have died?
...
Rest in peace, my poor comrade,
rest in peace; more sad is
the fate of your god than is yours.
The gods weep,
the gods weep when the dog dies
who licked their hands,
who looked into their eyes
and when looking in them thus asked:
where are we going?

Miguel de Unamuno y Jugo

THE HEAVEN OF ANIMALS

Here they are. The soft eyes open.
If they have lived in a wood
It is a wood.
If they have lived on plains
It is grass rolling
Under their feet forever.

Having no souls, they have come,
Anyway, beyond their knowing.
Their instincts wholly bloom
And they rise.
The soft eyes open.

To match them, the landscape flowers,
Outdoing, desperately
Outdoing what is required:
The richest wood,
The deepest field.

For some of these,
It could not be the place
It is, without blood.
These hunt, as they have done,
But with claws and teeth grown perfect,

More deadly than they can believe.
They stalk more silently,

And crouch on the limbs of trees,
And their descent
Upon the bright backs of their prey

May take years
In a sovereign floating of joy.
And those that are hunted
Know this as their life,
Their reward: to walk

Under such trees in full knowledge
Of what is in glory above them,
And to feel no fear,
But acceptance, compliance.
Fulfilling themselves without pain

At the cycle's center,
They tremble, they walk
Under the tree,
They fall, they are torn,
They rise, they walk again.

James Dickey

Thou grievest where no grief should be! Thou
     speak'st
Words lacking wisdom! For the wise in heart
Mourn not for those that live, nor those that die.
…
For ever and for ever afterwards.
All, that doth live, lives always!
…
The end of birth is death; the end of death
Is birth: this is ordained! …
What is there sorrowful herein?
This life within all living things, my Prince!
Hides beyond harm.

                    Bhagavad Gita, excerpts from chapter 2

BOX OF SOULS

O Creator,
carver of the box of souls
the one who nailed the four corners
of the universe and placed all beasts —
of land and sky and sea —
within the whittled wood.

O Creator,
carver of the box of souls,
the one who sends the sun
on her journey through the doors
at dawn and dusk.

O Creator,
carver of the box of souls,
the one who holds the sun above the house
each night — swimming as starlight,
through cracks in the roof.

O Creator,
carver of the box of souls,
your house shakes in the storm.
The back door is splintered, the sun gone.
And in the thunder of mourning,
a soul lifts in your wind.

O Creator,
carver of the box of souls,
receive this one who journeys from our house,
then send your sun back
to our door at dawn.

Lynn L. Caruso

This prayer is based on the Tsimshian belief that the
world is an enormous box or house containing all the
souls in the universe — animal and human alike.

PET MEMORIAL

We have come here today to honor and give thanks for a very special pet, [pet's name]. This creature of God holds a very special place in the hearts of the people gathered together here today. [Pet's name] made his [her] transition [date] and we come here to mark his [her] passing with a remembering of the gift he [she] was and the gifts he [she] brought into the lives he [she] touched. You that have come here today to remember [pet's name] are here because your life was no doubt made richer and fuller by having known this special furry loved one. Anyone who has had the honor of having a [type of companion animal] knows what it feels like to be trusted completely, forgiven immediately, and loved unconditionally.

I would like to invite any of you that would feel comfortable doing so to share with us for a few moments whatever memories you would like to share.

[Allow time for sharing.]

Thank you each for sharing your memories with us. God is love and God is life. We gathered here know that certainly [pet's name] is an expression of God's love and life. Though he [she] is not here physically any longer, his [her] essence, which is love, will always be with you.

Let us pray.

> Blessed Mother/Father Creator of all,
> We give grateful thanks for [pet's name].
> We give thanks that he [she] came wagging his [her] tail [adapt appropriately] into the lives of his [her] friends and family and by so doing made their lives richer and fuller.
> We hold his [her] memory lovingly in our hearts as we have released his [her] physical form.
> We give thanks for the lessons he [she] taught so patiently and lovingly.
> We are grateful for the time we were together in this life and know that the essence of [pet's name] lives on, for his [her] essence is love.
> As we grieve his [her] passing we celebrate his [her] life.
> We give thanks that he [she] chose [owner's name] to be his [her] people and in choosing them became an important member of their family.
> Being the people chosen by [pet's name] is a blessing that even now calls us to come up higher, to forgive more quickly, trust more easily, and love unconditionally.

Thank you, God, for your love so wonderfully
expressed in the being of [pet's name]. We
release our loved one into the care of a loving
God. Amen.

Rev. Gloria S. Moncrief

May the earth be soft under you when you rest upon it, tired at the end of a day, and may it rest lightly over you when at the last, you lay out under it; may it rest so lightly over you that your soul may be off from under it quickly and up and off, and on its way to God. And now may the Lord bless you all and bless you kindly.

Traditional Irish blessing

12 Benediction

When you walk across the fields with your mind pure and holy, then from all the stones, and all growing things, and all animals, the sparks of their soul come out and cling to you, and then they are purified and become a holy fire in you.

Hasidic saying

Ripe heads of barley
    Bent down by a rain,
    Bowing
Narrow my pathway

Joso

WOODLAND CARIBOU

Blessings of river reeds
 Bent down in their search for drink
 Bowing
They narrow your pathway

Blessings of mountain huckleberries
 Bent down with their heavy fruit
 Bowing
They narrow your pathway

Blessings of ancient cedar
 Bent down in a summer storm
 Bowing
They narrow your pathway

Blessings of scarlet fireweed
 Bent down in the tide of winds
 Bowing
They narrow your pathway

Blessings of human hands
 Bent down on this trail we share
 Bowing
We narrow your pathway

Lynn L. Caruso, after Joso

This poem arose from a desire to honor all endangered
species—"bowing" to surround them with a narrow path
of protection (see p. 239).

How lovely are thy holy groves
God of heaven and earth
My soul longs and faints
for the circle of thy trees.
My heart and my flesh
sing with joy to thee
O God of life.

May all things move and be moved in me
all know and be known in me
May all creation
dance for joy within me.

Chinook prayer

The deeper we look into nature, the more we recognize that it is full of life, and the more profoundly we know that all life is a secret and that we are united with all life that is in nature. Man can no longer live for himself alone. We realize that all life is valuable, and that we are united to all this life. From this knowledge comes our spiritual relationship to the universe.

Albert Schweitzer

Love all of God's creation, both the whole of it and every grain of sand. Love every leaf, every ray of God's light. Love animals, love plants, love each thing. If you love each thing, you will perceive the mystery of God in things. Once you have perceived it, you will begin tirelessly to perceive more and more of it every day. And you will come at last to love the whole world with an entire, universal love. Love the animals: God gave them the rudiments of thought and an untroubled joy. Do not trouble it, do not torment them, do not take their joy from them, do not go against God's purpose.

Fyodor Dostoevsky

And God said to Noah and to his sons with him, "I now establish My covenant with you and your offspring to come, and with every living thing that is with you—birds, cattle, and every wild beast as well—all that have come out of the ark, every living thing on earth."

...

God further said, "This is the sign that I set for the covenant between Me and you, and every living creature with you, for all ages to come. I have set My bow in the clouds, and it shall serve as a sign of the covenant between Me and the earth."

Genesis 9:8–10, 12–13

A PRAYER FOR PROTECTING ANIMALS

O God, source of life and power, Who feedeth the birds of the heavens, increase our tenderness towards all the creatures of Thy hand. Help us to refrain from petty acts of cruelty, or thoughtless deeds of harm to any living animal. May we care for them at all times, especially during hard weather, and protect them from injury so that they learn to trust us as friends.

Let our sympathy grow with knowledge, so that the whole creation may rejoice in Thy presence.

Author unknown

TO BE OF SERVICE

All creatures are created from the same paternal heartbeat of God. Not to hurt our humble brethren is our first duty to them, but to stop there is not enough. We have a higher mission—to be of service to them wherever they require it. If you have men who will exclude any of God's creatures from the shelter of compassion and pity, you will have men who will deal likewise with their fellow men.

St. Francis of Assisi

~

Until one has loved an animal, a part of one's soul remains unawakened.

Anatole France

~

Where the cuckoo's dark
Song crosses
The skylark's clear
High song, there am I!

Mukai Kyorai

In one salutation to thee, my God, let
all my senses spread out and touch this
world at thy feet.

…

Like a flock of homesick cranes flying
night and day back to their mountain
nests let all my life take its voyage to
its eternal home in one salutation to
thee.

Rabindranath Tagore, Gitanjali *103*

⁓

Be my benediction said
With my hand upon thy head,
Gentle fellow-creature.

Eliza Lee Cabot Follen

A LIMB JUST MOVED

You taught Your songs to the birds first,
    why is that?
And You practiced Your love in the hearts of
      animals before You created man.
I know all the planets talk at night and tell
      secrets about You.
A limb just moved before me, and the beauty of
      this world is causing me to weep.

Mirabai

EAGLE POEM

To pray you open your whole self
To sky, to earth, to sun, to moon
To one whole voice that is you.
And know there is more
That you can't see, can't hear,
Can't know except in moments
Steadily growing, and in languages
That aren't always sound but other
Circles of motion.
Like eagle that Sunday morning
Over Salt River. Circled in blue sky
In wind, swept our hearts clean
With sacred wings.
We see you, see ourselves and know
That we must take the utmost care
And kindness in all things.
Breathe in, knowing we are made of
All this, and breathe, knowing
We are truly blessed because we
Were born, and die soon within a
True circle of motion,
Like eagle rounding out the morning

Inside us.
We pray that it will be done
In beauty.
In beauty.

Joy Harjo

About the Contributors

Akhenaton (reigned 1366–1349 BCE), Egyptian pharaoh, also known as Amenhotep IV, who introduced a form of monotheism in religion.

Alexander, Cecil Frances (1818–1895), Irish hymn writer and poet best known for her hymn "All Things Bright and Beautiful."

Bashō, Matsuo (1644–1694), Japanese poet who brought haiku to its highest level and whose work appeals to the modern reader.

Beecher, Henry Ward (1813–1887), American clergyman who was popular for his sermons that addressed current events and social reform.

Bergh, Henry (1811–1888), founder of the American Society for the Prevention of Cruelty to Animals (ASPCA).

Besant, Annie (1847–1933), English theosophist, social reformer, and leader of India's independence movement.

Bierce, Ambrose (1842–1914), American journalist and author known for his Civil War stories.

Black Elk (1863–1950), Oglala Lakota Sioux holy man and author of *Black Elk Speaks*.

Browning, Elizabeth Barrett (1806–1861), English poet whose best-known work is *Sonnets from the Portuguese*.

Buber, Martin (1878–1965), Jewish philosopher born in Vienna and author of *I and Thou* and *The Tales of the Hasidim*.

Buson, Yosa (1716–1784), Japanese poet known for his revival of haiku; a major painter.

223

Caruso, Isaac, six-year-old student from Spokane, Washington, who loves riding his bike and camping. This is his very first poem.

Chang Chiu-Ch'eng, Chinese classical Zen (Ch'an) poet of the T'ang dynasty.

Chendo, John C., poet and interfaith chaplain to persons with developmental disabilities; a graduate of Union Theological Seminary and NYU School of Law. He lives in Davis, California.

Chesterton, Gilbert Keith (1874–1936), English writer, poet, and essayist; best known for his popular detective stories of Father Brown.

Chih, Feng (1905–1993), considered one of the most important lyric poets in China; known especially for his sonnets.

Ciardi, John (1918–1986), American poet and critic influential in his role as poetry editor of the *Saturday Review.*

Cocteau, Jean (1889–1963), French writer, artist, poet, and filmmaker; best known for his artistic ballets.

Cowdell, Rev. Dr. Scott, rector of St. Paul's Anglican Church in Canberra, Australia, and theology professor at Charles Sturt University. His latest book is *God's Next Big Thing: Discovering the Future Church.*

Dickey, James (1923–1997), American poet, winner of the 1965 National Book Award in poetry, and author of the novel *Deliverance.*

Dickinson, Emily (1830–1886), American poet; widely considered one of the greatest poets in American literature.

Doane, George Washington (1799–1859), Episcopal bishop of New Jersey and author of numerous hymns.

Dostoevsky, Fyodor (1821–1881), Russian novelist who was influential in the development of the modern novel.

Doty, Mark, contemporary American prize-winning poet whose work celebrates living things of all kinds.

Eckhart, Johann (c. 1260–1328), known as Meister Eckhart, theologian who founded mysticism in Germany.

Farrell, Mary Cronk, children's author and family spirituality columnist whose recent publications include *Celebrating Faith: Year-Round Activities for Catholic Families* and her coauthored work *Daughters of the Desert: Stories of Remarkable Women from Christian, Jewish and Muslim Traditions* (SkyLight Paths).

Feister, John Bookser, director of the Internet department at St. Anthony Messenger Press (www.AmericanCatholic.org) and managing editor of *Catholic Update.*

Finkelstein, Rev. Roberta, interim minister of the Unitarian Universalist Congregation of Frederick, Maryland. She shares her home with her husband, son, and many companion animals.

Follen, Eliza Lee Cabot (1787–1860), popular American author of poems, plays, and stories for children.

Foulk, T. Griffith, author of numerous articles and the forthcoming *Ch'an Myths and Realities in Medieval Chinese Buddhism.* Professor of religion at Sarah Lawrence College.

France, Anatole (1844–1924), French novelist, critic, poet, and playwright who won the Nobel Prize for literature in 1921.

Francis of Assisi, Saint (c. 1181–1226), Christian saint who founded the Franciscan religious order and is known for his love of all creatures.

Guerrero, Diana L., writer and animal behaviorist active in the zoological community and humane organizations; author of *What Animals Can Teach Us about Spirituality: Inspiring Lessons from Wild and Tame Creatures* (SkyLight Paths).

Harjo, Joy, writer, poet, artist, screenwriter, and musician; a member of the Muskogee tribe; born in Oklahoma.

Hauerwas, Stanley, United Methodist theologian, ethicist, and distinguished professor who teaches at Duke Divinity School in Durham, North Carolina.

Heffernan, Kathy, a pastoral counselor, reiki teacher, and writer living in Seattle, Washington, who uses poetry in her classes and pastoral counseling sessions to connect spirituality, creativity, and healing.

Hirshfield, Jane, contemporary American prize-winning poet, writer, and translator.

Hokanson, Alicia, poet and teacher from Seattle, Washington. Her three collections of poetry are *Phosphorous, Mapping the Distance,* and *Insistent in the Skin.*

Hopkins, Gerard Manley (1844–1889), English Jesuit priest whose lyrical, spiritual poetry reflected his view of poetry as an "inner landscape."

Hugo, Victor (1802–1885), French poet, novelist, and playwright; author of *Les Misérables.*

Issa, Kobayashi (1763–1823), Japanese haiku poet of the late Tokugawa period.

Jammes, Francis (1868–1938), French poet and novelist, well-known for his rustic themes.

John of the Cross, Saint (1542–1591), Christian mystical philosopher and writer.

Joso, Naito (1660–1704), Japanese haiku poet of the Tokugawa period.

Kabir (1440–1518), mystical Hindu poet in India who was influenced by the mystic Sufi branch of Islam.

Kinnell, Galway, American poet known for his images of the sacred in the natural world; winner of both the Pulitzer Prize and the National Book Award.

Kipling, Rudyard (1865–1936), English poet, novelist, and short-story writer famous for his tales of India.

Klein, Laurie, award-winning songwriter and poet whose collection of poems is *Bodies of Water, Bodies of Flesh.* She is a founding editor of *Rock & Sling: A Journal of Literature, Art, and Faith.*

Kyorai, Mukai (1651–1704), Japanese haiku poet and disciple of Bashō.

Lamon, Laurie, associate professor of English at Whitworth College in Spokane, Washington. Her collection of poems is *The Fork without Hunger* from CavanKerry Press.

Lao-Tzu (born c. 600 BCE), Chinese philosopher known for his treatise *Tao Te Ching,* a basis for the Taoist religion and a work that was also very influential in Zen Buddhism.

Lawrence, D. H. (1885–1930), English novelist, poet, short-story writer, and essayist who profoundly influenced modern English fiction.

Lehnert, Richard, writer and freelance editor whose first book of poems, *A Short History of the Usual,* published in 2003, won the Readers' Choice award from Backwaters Press.

Letakos-Lesa (Eagle Chief), nineteenth-century Native American of the Pawnee tribe.

Lindholdt, Paul, English professor at Eastern Washington University and author of some 150 published books, articles, essays, poems, and newspaper stories; recipient of the First Place Award from the Academy of American Poets.

Mackin, Kevin E., OFM, president of Siena College in Loudonville, New York, educator, and author of *In Search of the Authentic Christian Tradition.*

MacManus, Seumas (1869–1960), Irish poet, historian, and novelist.

McLaughlin, Lauren, ordained Unity minister, serving God through Bless the Animals, an Internet prayer ministry at www.godblesstheanimals.com.

McLeod, Fiona (pseudonym of William Sharp), writer of Celtic visionary and mystic poetry in the late nineteenth century.

Michizane, Sugawara no (845–903), Japanese statesman honored by the tenth-century Kitano Shrine in Kyoto.

Mirabai (c. 1498–1550), the most celebrated female poet-saint of India. She was born a princess yet spent many years caring for the destitute.

Moncrief, Rev. Gloria S., senior minister at Unity Church of Indianapolis; she wrote "the pet memorial" for Spot, an English pointer who helped raise her two children and teach them the meaning of love and life.

Muir, John (1838–1914), American naturalist, explorer, and pioneering conservationist.

Murphy, Claire Rudolf, author of fifteen books for children and young adults. Her recent publications include *Children of Alcatraz* and her coauthored work, *Daughters of the Desert: Stories of Remarkable Women from Christian, Jewish and Muslim Traditions* (SkyLight Paths).

Pinsker, Gloria, professional dog trainer, portrait artist, and freelance writer residing in Horsham, Pennsylvania. She has published extensively and runs the Pet Prayer Line on the Internet.

Po Chü-i (772–846), prolific Chinese poet of the T'ang dynasty.

Ramakrishna, Sri (1836–1886), Hindu spiritual teacher and mystic known as "the God-man of India."

Reinke, Pam, American artist and writer who works out of her studio in Lake Havasu City, Arizona.

Rivage (pseudonym of Mary Newman), poet and visual artist residing in Davis, California. She strongly believes in the power of that shared Spirit with which each natural entity is imbued.

Rossetti, Christina (1830–1894), British poet closely connected to the Pre-Raphaelite Brotherhood (group of spiritual painters).

Rumi, Jalaluddin (1207–1273), mystic philosopher who founded the Mevlevi Order of Sufism.

Sandburg, Carl (1878–1967), American poet of the Midwest and Pulitzer Prize–winning biographer of Abraham Lincoln.

Sayres, Meghan Nuttall, tapestry weaver and author of *The Shape of Betts Meadow: A Wetlands Story* and coauthor of *Daughters of the Desert: Tales of Remarkable Women from Christian, Jewish and Muslim Traditions* (SkyLight Paths). Her novel, *Anahita's Woven Riddle*, is forthcoming.

Schweitzer, Albert (1875–1965), Nobel laureate, humanitarian, theologian, scholar, and physician whose central message was "reverence for life."

Scott, Sir Walter (1771–1832), Scottish poet and novelist known for his narrative poems and historical fiction.

Shiki, Masaoka (1867–1902), Japanese poet who infused traditional haiku with a new naturalistic aesthetic.

Shikibu, Izumi (c. 974–1033), Japanese poet whose works were included in imperial anthologies and preserved in memoirs.

Sisk, Mark S., fifteenth Episcopal bishop of New York and former dean of Seabury-Western Seminary.

Smart, Christopher (1722–1771), English poet and translator best known for his religious poem "A Song to David."

Tagore, Rabindranath (1861–1941), Indian poet, philosopher, and social reformer who won the Nobel Prize in literature.

Thoreau, Henry David (1817–1862), American author best known for his book *Walden* and for his embrace of nature and transcendentalism.

Twain, Mark (1835–1910), pseudonym of Samuel Clemens, American writer and humorist; best known for *The Adventures of Huckleberry Finn*.

Unamuno y Jugo, Miguel de (1864–1936), Spanish author and philosopher whose writings on religion and existentialism were influential in early twentieth-century Spain.

Underhill, Evelyn (1875–1941), English writer and spiritual thinker; author of the influential *Mysticism*.

Van Vechten, Carl (1880–1964), American writer and photographer.

White, Rabbi Harold S., senior Jewish chaplain and theology lecturer at Georgetown University; active in interfaith ministry.

Whitman, Walt (1819–1892), American poet known for his sensual imagery, personal religion, and egalitarianism.

Wright, James Arlington (1927–1980), American poet and translator who won the Pulitzer Prize in 1972.

Yeats, William Butler (1865–1939), Irish poet, dramatist, and essayist who was instrumental in the early twentieth-century Irish literary revival.

Credits

Grateful acknowledgment is given for the use of material included in this book. An exhaustive effort has been made to obtain the necessary permissions to use copyrighted material. If any material has been unintentionally used without proper permission, please contact the editor and we will ensure appropriate credit is acknowledged in future editions.

Many thanks to the editors of the following magazines in which these poems first appeared, and to the authors who generously granted permission to reprint them:

The Atlantic Monthly, "Praise" by Laurie Lamon; *Crux*, "Where the Sky Opens" by Laurie Klein; *Jeopardy*, "The Way to Open" by Paul Lindholdt; *The Melbourne Anglican*, "Animal Care and the New Creation" by Rev. Dr. Scott Cowdell; *Self Portrait; Poetry on the Buses*, "Summer in the Methow" by Kathy Heffernan; *The Sun*, "Essay on Compassion" by Richard Lehnert; *Tricycle: The Buddhist Review*, quote beginning, "All sentient beings ..." by T. Griffith Foulk.

We sincerely appreciate the permissions so generously granted by the listed authors and rightsholders:

"Birds Make Great Sky Circles," reprinted with permission of translator, Coleman Barks. Originally published in *The Essential Rumi* by HarperCollins, 1995.

Excerpts from "Elegy on the Death of a Dog" in *Poems of Miguel de Unamuno y Jugo*, translated by Eleanor L. Turnbull, pp. 102–109. © 1952 Eleanor L. Turnbull. Reprinted with permission of The Johns Hopkins University Press.

Quotes beginning, "We give you thanks ..." and "Live without fear ..." both by Bishop Mark S. Sisk, reprinted from "St. Francis at St. John the Divine" by Jack Wintz, OFM, St. Anthony Messenger Magazine Online, © 2003. Used by permission of St. Anthony Messenger Press, 28 W. Liberty St., Cincinnati, OH 45202; 800-488-0488. www.AmericanCatholic.org All rights reserved.

"Prayer" by Rabbi Harold S. White excerpted from *We Thank You, God, for These: Blessings and Prayers for Family Pets* by Anthony F. Chiffolo and Rayner W. Hesse Jr., Copyright © 2003, Paulist Press, Inc., New York/Mahwah, N.J. Used with permission of Paulist Press. www.paulistpress.com or call 800-218-1903

James Wright, "A Blessing," from *The Branch Will Not Break* © 1963 James Wright and reprinted by permission of Wesleyan University Press.

The following translations of sacred texts were used throughout this book:

Alī, Abdullah Yūsuf. *The Meaning of the Holy Qur'an*. Beltsville, Md.: Amana Publications, 1999, 2003.

Griffith, Ralph T. H., trans. *Rig Veda*. Chicago: Vivekananda Vedanta Society, 1896.

Holy Bible: New Revised Standard Version. Nashville: Holman Bible Publishers, 1989.

Mukerji, Dhan Gopal, trans. *The Song of God*. New York: E. P. Dutton & Co., 1931.

Sutta Nipata. London: Royal Asiatic Society, 1894.

Swami, Shri Purohit, trans. *The Bhagavad Gita: Annotated and Explained*. Woodstock, Vt.: SkyLight Paths Publishing, 2001.

Tanakh: A New Translation of the Holy Scriptures According to the Traditional Hebrew Text. Philadelphia: Jewish Publication Society, 1985.

Acknowledgments

Special thanks to Don and Doris Liebert for your limitless support; Anna Caruso; my writing group: Mary Douthitt, Mary Cronk Farrell, Claire Rudolf Murphy, and my sincere gratitude to Meghan Nuttall Sayres for introducing me to Maura D. Shaw, my tireless editor. And to Sarah McBride, at SkyLight Paths, for seeing the project through.

Editor's Note

Just north of my family's cabin in the Selkirk Mountains is the temperate rainforest of northern Idaho. It was once home to a thriving population of woodland (or mountain) caribou, but recent surveys have determined that only three caribou remain in the mountains of Idaho. These shocking numbers make the woodland caribou the most endangered mammal in the United States. To learn more about the plight of the woodland caribou, visit the Washington Department of Fish and Wildlife at http://wdfw.wa.gov/wlm/research/caribou/caribou.htm or the Lands Council's website at http://www.lands council.org.

Prayer / Meditation

Sacred Attention: A Spiritual Practice for Finding God in the Moment
by Margaret D. McGee
Framed on the Christian liturgical year, this inspiring guide explores ways to develop a practice of attention as a means of talking—and listening—to God.
6 x 9, 144 pp, HC, 978-1-59473-232-4 **$19.99**

Women Pray: Voices through the Ages, from Many Faiths, Cultures and Traditions
Edited and with Introductions by Monica Furlong
5 x 7¼, 256 pp, Quality PB, 978-1-59473-071-9 **$15.99**

Women of Color Pray: Voices of Strength, Faith, Healing, Hope and Courage *Edited and with Introductions by Christal M. Jackson*
Through these prayers, poetry, lyrics, meditations and affirmations, you will share in the strong and undeniable connection women of color share with God.
5 x 7¼, 208 pp, Quality PB, 978-1-59473-077-1 **$15.99**

Secrets of Prayer: A Multifaith Guide to Creating Personal Prayer in Your Life *by Nancy Corcoran, CSJ*
This compelling, multifaith guidebook offers you companionship and encouragement on the journey to a healthy prayer life. 6 x 9, 160 pp, Quality PB, 978-1-59473-215-7 **$16.99**

Prayers to an Evolutionary God
by William Cleary; Afterword by Diarmuid O'Murchu
Inspired by the spiritual and scientific teachings of Diarmuid O'Murchu and Teilhard de Chardin, reveals that religion and science can be combined to create an expanding view of the universe—an evolutionary faith.
6 x 9, 208 pp, HC, 978-1-59473-006-1 **$21.99**

The Art of Public Prayer: Not for Clergy Only *by Lawrence A. Hoffman*
6 x 9, 288 pp, Quality PB, 978-1-893361-06-5 **$18.99**

A Heart of Stillness: A Complete Guide to Learning the Art of Meditation
by David A. Cooper 5½ x 8½, 272 pp, Quality PB, 978-1-893361-03-4 **$16.95**

Meditation without Gurus: A Guide to the Heart of Practice
by Clark Strand 5½ x 8½, 192 pp, Quality PB, 978-1-893361-93-5 **$16.95**

Praying with Our Hands: 21 Practices of Embodied Prayer from the World's Spiritual Traditions *by Jon M. Sweeney; Photographs by Jennifer J. Wilson; Foreword by Mother Tessa Bielecki; Afterword by Taitetsu Unno, PhD*
8 x 8, 96 pp, 22 duotone photos, Quality PB, 978-1-893361-16-4 **$16.95**

Silence, Simplicity & Solitude: A Complete Guide to Spiritual Retreat at Home
by David A. Cooper 5½ x 8½, 336 pp, Quality PB, 978-1-893361-04-1 **$16.95**

Three Gates to Meditation Practice: A Personal Journey into Sufism, Buddhism, and Judaism *by David A. Cooper* 5½ x 8½, 240 pp, Quality PB, 978-1-893361-22-5 **$16.95**

Spirituality

Next to Godliness: Finding the Sacred in Housekeeping
Edited and with Introductions by Alice Peck Offers new perspectives on how we can reach
out for the Divine. 6 x 9, 224 pp, Quality PB, 978-1-59473-214-0 **$19.99**

Bread, Body, Spirit: Finding the Sacred in Food
Edited and with Introductions by Alice Peck
Explores how food feeds our faith. 6 x 9, 224 pp, Quality PB, 978-1-59473-242-3 **$19.99**

Renewal in the Wilderness: A Spiritual Guide to Connecting with
God in the Natural World *by John Lionberger*
Reveals the power of experiencing God's presence in many variations of the nat-
ural world. 6 x 9, 176 pp, b/w photos, Quality PB, 978-1-59473-219-5 **$16.99**

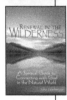

Honoring Motherhood: Prayers, Ceremonies and Blessings
Edited and with Introductions by Lynn L. Caruso
Journey through the seasons of motherhood. 5 x 7¼, 272 pp, HC, 978-1-59473-239-3 **$19.99**

Soul Fire: Accessing Your Creativity *by Rev. Thomas Ryan, CSP*
Learn to cultivate your creative spirit. 6 x 9, 160 pp, Quality PB, 978-1-59473-243-0 **$16.99**

Technology & Spirituality: How the Information Revolution Affects
Our Spiritual Lives *by Stephen K. Spyker* 6 x 9, 176 pp, HC, 978-1-59473-218-8 **$19.99**

Money and the Way of Wisdom: Insights from the Book of Proverbs
by Timothy J. Sandoval, PhD 6 x 9, 192 pp (est), Quality PB, 978-1-59473-245-4 **$16.99**

Awakening the Spirit, Inspiring the Soul
30 Stories of Interspiritual Discovery in the Community of Faiths
Edited by Brother Wayne Teasdale and Martha Howard, MD; Foreword by Joan Borysenko, PhD
6 x 9, 224 pp, HC, 978-1-59473-039-1 **$21.99**

Creating a Spiritual Retirement: A Guide to the Unseen Possibilities in Our Lives
by Molly Srode 6 x 9, 208 pp, b/w photos, Quality PB, 978-1-59473-050-4 **$14.99**
HC, 978-1-893361-75-1 **$19.95**

Finding Hope: Cultivating God's Gift of a Hopeful Spirit
by Marcia Ford 8 x 8, 200 pp, Quality PB, 978-1-59473-211-9 **$16.99**

The Geography of Faith: Underground Conversations on Religious, Political and Social
Change *by Daniel Berrigan and Robert Coles* 6 x 9, 224 pp, Quality PB, 978-1-893361-40-9 **$16.95**

Jewish Spirituality: A Brief Introduction for Christians *by Lawrence Kushner*
5½ x 8½, 112 pp, Quality PB, 978-1-58023-150-3 **$12.95** *(a Jewish Lights book)*

Journeys of Simplicity: Traveling Light with Thomas Merton, Bashō, Edward
Abbey, Annie Dillard & Others *by Philip Harnden*
5 x 7¼, 144 pp, Quality PB, 978-1-59473-181-5 **$12.99** 128 pp, HC, 978-1-893361-76-8 **$16.95**

Keeping Spiritual Balance As We Grow Older: More than 65 Creative Ways to
Use Purpose, Prayer, and the Power of Spirit to Build a Meaningful Retirement
by Molly and Bernie Srode 8 x 8, 224 pp, Quality PB, 978-1-59473-042-9 **$16.99**

Spirituality 101: The Indispensable Guide to Keeping—or Finding—Your Spiritual
Life on Campus *by Harriet L. Schwartz, with contributions from college students at nearly thirty
campuses across the United States* 6 x 9, 272 pp, Quality PB, 978-1-59473-000-9 **$16.99**

Spiritually Incorrect: Finding God in All the Wrong Places *by Dan Wakefield; Illus. by
Marian DelVecchio* 5½ x 8½, 192 pp, b/w illus., Quality PB, 978-1-59473-137-2 **$15.99**

Spiritual Manifestos: Visions for Renewed Religious Life in America from Young
Spiritual Leaders of Many Faiths *Edited by Niles Elliot Goldstein; Preface by Martin E. Marty*
6 x 9, 256 pp, HC, 978-1-893361-09-6 **$21.95**

A Walk with Four Spiritual Guides: Krishna, Buddha, Jesus, and Ramakrishna
by Andrew Harvey 5½ x 8½, 192 pp, 10 b/w photos & illus., Quality PB, 978-1-59473-138-9 **$15.99**

What Matters: Spiritual Nourishment for Head and Heart
by Frederick Franck 5 x 7¼, 128 pp, 50+ b/w illus., HC, 978-1-59473-013-9 **$16.99**

Who Is My God?, 2nd Edition: An Innovative Guide to Finding Your Spiritual Identity
Created by the Editors at SkyLight Paths 6 x 9, 160 pp, Quality PB, 978-1-59473-014-6 **$15.99**

Judaism / Christianity / Interfaith

Talking about God: Exploring the Meaning of Religious Life with Kierkegaard, Buber, Tillich and Heschel *by Daniel F. Polish, PhD*
Examines the meaning of the human religious experience with the greatest theologians of modern times. 6 x 9, 160 pp, HC, 978-1-59473-230-0 **$21.99**

Interactive Faith: The Essential Interreligious Community-Building Handbook
Edited by Rev. Bud Heckman with Rori Picker Neiss
A guide to the key methods and resources of the interfaith movement.
6 x 9, 304 pp, HC, 978-1-59473-237-9 **$29.99**

The Jewish Approach to Repairing the World (*Tikkun Olam*)
A Brief Introduction for Christians *by Rabbi Elliot N. Dorff, PhD, and Reverend Cory Willson*
A window into the Jewish idea of responsibility to care for the world.
5½ x 8½, 256 pp, 978-1-58023-349-1 **$16.99** (a Jewish Lights book)

Modern Jews Engage the New Testament: Enhancing Jewish Well-Being in a Christian Environment *by Rabbi Michael J. Cook, PhD*
A look at the dynamics of the New Testament.
6 x 9, 416 pp, HC, 978-1-58023-313-2 **$29.99** (a Jewish Lights book)

Disaster Spiritual Care: Practical Clergy Responses to Community, Regional and National Tragedy
Edited by Rabbi Stephen B. Roberts, BCJC, & Rev. Willard W.C. Ashley, Sr., DMin, DH
The definitive reference for pastoral caregivers of all faiths involved in disaster response.
6 x 9, 384 pp, Hardcover, 978-1-59473-240-9 **$40.00**

The Changing Christian World: A Brief Introduction for Jews
by Rabbi Leonard A. Schoolman
5½ x 8½, 176 pp, Quality PB, 978-1-58023-344-6 **$16.99** (a Jewish Lights book)

The Jewish Connection to Israel, the Promised Land: A Brief Introduction for Christians *by Rabbi Eugene Korn, PhD*
5½ x 8½, 192 pp, Quality PB, 978-1-58023-318-7 **$14.99** (a Jewish Lights book)

Christians and Jews in Dialogue: Learning in the Presence of the Other
by Mary C. Boys and Sara S. Lee; Foreword by Dorothy C. Bass
Inspires renewed commitment to dialogue between religious traditions.
6 x 9, 240 pp, HC, 978-1-59473-144-0 **$21.99**

Healing the Jewish-Christian Rift: Growing Beyond Our Wounded History
by Ron Miller and Laura Bernstein; Foreword by Dr. Beatrice Bruteau
6 x 9, 288 pp, Quality PB, 978-1-59473-139-6 **$18.99**

Introducing My Faith and My Community
The Jewish Outreach Institute Guide for the Christian in a Jewish Interfaith Relationship
by Rabbi Kerry M. Olitzky 6 x 9, 176 pp, Quality PB, 978-1-58023-192-3 **$16.99** *(a Jewish Lights book)*

The Jewish Approach to God: A Brief Introduction for Christians
by Rabbi Neil Gillman 5½ x 8½, 192 pp, Quality PB, 978-1-58023-190-9 **$16.95** *(a Jewish Lights book)*

Jewish Holidays: A Brief Introduction for Christians
by Rabbi Kerry M. Olitzky and Rabbi Daniel Judson
5½ x 8½, 176 pp, Quality PB, 978-1-58023-302-6 **$16.99** *(a Jewish Lights book)*

Jewish Ritual: A Brief Introduction for Christians
by Rabbi Kerry M. Olitzky and Rabbi Daniel Judson
5½ x 8½, 144 pp, Quality PB, 978-1-58023-210-4 **$14.99** *(a Jewish Lights book)*

Jewish Spirituality: A Brief Introduction for Christians *by Rabbi Lawrence Kushner*
5½ x 8½, 112 pp, Quality PB, 978-1-58023-150-3 **$12.95** *(a Jewish Lights book)*

A Jewish Understanding of the New Testament
by Rabbi Samuel Sandmel; new Preface by Rabbi David Sandmel
5½ x 8½, 368 pp, Quality PB, 978-1-59473-048-1 **$19.99**

We Jews and Jesus: Exploring Theological Differences for Mutual Understanding
by Rabbi Samuel Sandmel; new Preface by Rabbi David Sandmel A Classic Reprint
6 x 9, 192 pp, Quality PB, 978-1-59473-208-9 **$16.99**

Show Me Your Way: The Complete Guide to Exploring Interfaith Spiritual Direction
by Howard A. Addison 5½ x 8½, 240 pp, Quality PB, 978-1-893361-41-6 **$16.95**

Spiritual Poetry—The Mystic Poets

Experience these mystic poets as you never have before. Each beautiful, compact book includes: a brief introduction to the poet's time and place; a summary of the major themes of the poet's mysticism and religious tradition; essential selections from the poet's most important works; and an appreciative preface by a contemporary spiritual writer.

Hafiz
The Mystic Poets
Preface by Ibrahim Gamard
Hafiz is known throughout the world as Persia's greatest poet, with sales of his poems in Iran today only surpassed by those of the Qur'an itself. His probing and joyful verse speaks to people from all backgrounds who long to taste and feel divine love and experience harmony with all living things.
5 x 7¼, 144 pp, HC, 978-1-59473-009-2 **$16.99**

Hopkins
The Mystic Poets
Preface by Rev. Thomas Ryan, CSP
Gerard Manley Hopkins, Christian mystical poet, is beloved for his use of fresh language and startling metaphors to describe the world around him. Although his verse is lovely, beneath the surface lies a searching soul, wrestling with and yearning for God.
5 x 7¼, 112 pp, HC, 978-1-59473-010-8 **$16.99**

Tagore
The Mystic Poets
Preface by Swami Adiswarananda
Rabindranath Tagore is often considered the "Shakespeare" of modern India. A great mystic, Tagore was the teacher of W. B. Yeats and Robert Frost, the close friend of Albert Einstein and Mahatma Gandhi, and the winner of the Nobel Prize for Literature. This beautiful sampling of Tagore's two most important works, *The Gardener* and *Gitanjali,* offers a glimpse into his spiritual vision that has inspired people around the world.
5 x 7¼, 144 pp, HC, 978-1-59473-008-5 **$16.99**

Whitman
The Mystic Poets
Preface by Gary David Comstock
Walt Whitman was the most innovative and influential poet of the nineteenth century. This beautiful sampling of Whitman's most important poetry from *Leaves of Grass,* and selections from his prose writings, offers a glimpse into the spiritual side of his most radical themes—love for country, love for others, and love of Self.
5 x 7¼, 192 pp, HC, 978-1-59473-041-2 **$16.99**

Journeys of Simplicity
Traveling Light with Thomas Merton, Bashō,
Edward Abbey, Annie Dillard & Others
Invites you to consider a more graceful way of traveling through life.
Use the included journal pages (in PB only) to help you get started on
your own spiritual journey.

Ed. by Philip Harnden
5 x 7¼, 144 pp, Quality PB, 978-1-59473-181-5 **$12.99**
5 x 7¼, 128 pp, HC, 978-1-893361-76-8 **$16.95**

Spirituality & Crafts

The Knitting Way
A Guide to Spiritual Self-Discovery
by Linda Skolnik and Janice MacDaniels
Examines how you can explore and strengthen your spiritual life through knitting.
7 x 9, 240 pp, Quality PB, b/w photographs, 978-1-59473-079-5 **$16.99**

The Scrapbooking Journey
A Hands-On Guide to Spiritual Discovery
by Cory Richardson-Lauve; Foreword by Stacy Julian
Reveals how this craft can become a practice used to deepen and shape your life.
7 x 9, 176 pp, Quality PB, 8-page full-color insert, plus b/w photographs
978-1-59473-216-4 **$18.99**

The Painting Path
Embodying Spiritual Discovery through Yoga, Brush and Color
by Linda Novick; Foreword by Richard Segalman
Explores the divine connection you can experience through creativity.
7 x 9, 208 pp, 8-page full-color insert, plus b/w photographs
Quality PB, 978-1-59473-226-3 **$18.99**

The Quilting Path
A Guide to Spiritual Discovery through Fabric, Thread and Kabbalah
by Louise Silk
Explores how to cultivate personal growth through quilt making.
7 x 9, 192 pp, Quality PB, b/w photographs and illustrations, 978-1-59473-206-5 **$16.99**

Contemplative Crochet
A Hands-On Guide for Interlocking Faith and Craft
by Cindy Crandall-Frazier; Foreword by Linda Skolnik
Illuminates the spiritual lessons you can learn through crocheting.
7 x 9, 192 pp (est), b/w photographs, Quality PB, 978-1-59473-238-6 **$16.99**

Kabbalah / Enneagram
(from Jewish Lights Publishing)

God in Your Body: Kabbalah, Mindfulness and Embodied Spiritual Practice
by Jay Michaelson 6 x 9, Quality PB Original, 978-1-58023-304-0 **$18.99**

Cast in God's Image: Discover Your Personality Type Using the Enneagram and Kabbalah
by Rabbi Howard A. Addison 7 x 9, 176 pp, Quality PB, 978-1-58023-124-4 **$16.95**

Ehyeh: A Kabbalah for Tomorrow *by Dr. Arthur Green*
6 x 9, 224 pp, Quality PB, 978-1-58023-213-5 **$16.99**

The Enneagram and Kabbalah, 2nd Edition: Reading Your Soul
by Rabbi Howard A. Addison 6 x 9, 192 pp, Quality PB, 978-1-58023-229-6 **$16.99**

The Gift of Kabbalah: Discovering the Secrets of Heaven, Renewing Your Life on Earth
by Tamar Frankiel, PhD 6 x 9, 256 pp, Quality PB, 978-1-58023-141-1 **$16.95**
HC, 978-1-58023-108-4 **$21.95**

Kabbalah: A Brief Introduction for Christians
by Tamar Frankiel, PhD 5½ x 8½, 176 pp, Quality PB, 978-1-58023-303-3 **$16.99**

Zohar: Annotated & Explained *Translation and Annotation by Dr. Daniel C. Matt*
Foreword by Andrew Harvey 5½ x 8½, 176 pp, Quality PB, 978-1-893361-51-5 **$15.99**
(a SkyLight Paths book)